The Drinkers' Guide
to the Middle East

The Drinkers' Guide to the Middle East

Will Lawson

Illustrated by Alex MacLeod

First published in Great Britain in 1997
by Rebel Inc., an imprint of Canongate Books Ltd,
14 High Street, Edinburgh EH1 1TE

Extract from 'The Diary of an Unknown Soldier' reproduced
by kind permission of The Stake magazine (Issue 2 1992 III
Publishing, PO Box 170363 San Francisco, CA 94117–0363)

British Library Cataloguing-in-Publication Data

A catalogue record for this book is available on request
from the British Library

ISBN 0 86241 703 1

Typeset in Fournier and Lebensjoy by
Palimpsest Book Production Limited,
Polmont, Stirlingshire

Printed and bound in Denmark by Norhaven A/S Rotation

for

The Regal

Contents

Acknowledgments

In Cairo, Fawzi Samir Hamed and Mahmud made my stay memorable and are working in the best bar in the Middle East. If you find it you are a clever reader between the lines and deserve to. Buy the guys a drink if you are feeling flush, they really deserve it. Georges is the man to clean your shoes – a deeply nice man. Buy your nuts from the tall stately bloke who is paying his way through university in this unusual manner. If he's at college, then the very nervous man with a paper bag full of nuts is a real sweetheart. Pen run out? Buy one or, better, several from the elvish little man who sells Reynolds Hi Fi pens. Why not? Flogging pens round Egyptian bars is hardly the most cheerful of occupations. Dr Adel provided much entertainment. Barking mad, but a gentleman. Thanks also to those pretty people who saved me from an unremitting diet of aesthetically challenged Egyptian alcoholics, principally Henry, Jon and Alison. Thanks to Mohammed for helping me with the Arabic, especially the vegetarian phrase.

In Edinburgh thanks are due to Robbie J— and Iain A— for technical assistance. And to Emma, Katherine Beba and Simon, for not barring me even when I do get phosphorescently drunk in their nice pub. Also to anyone who has been forced to read sections of this book while I was writing it, your patience and comments (apart from the abusive ones) were much appreciated.

Particularly Lesley Robinson, Chis Atton, Dave Scott, Russell Ellis, Peter Scott and James Mavor. And most of all to Emily Dewhurst for editing a completely straggle-witted text into something which made some kind of sense. (Well, it fooled the publishers.)

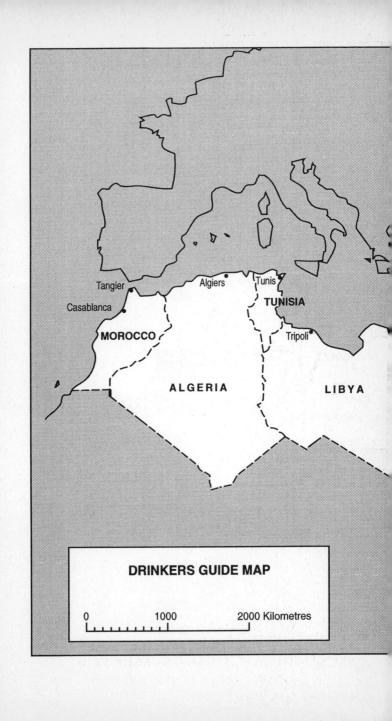

Tangier

Casablanca

Algiers

Tunis

TUNISIA

Tripoli

MOROCCO

ALGERIA

LIBYA

DRINKERS GUIDE MAP

0   1000   2000 Kilometres

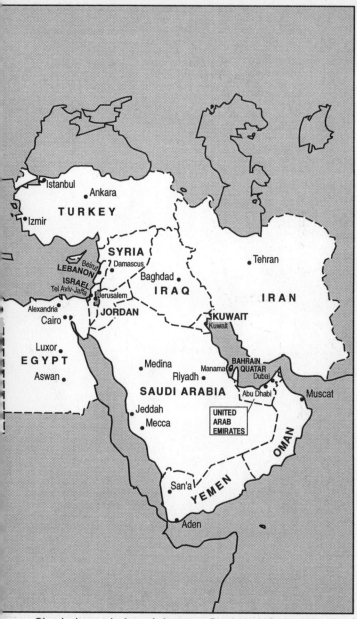

Shaded area in Israel denotes Occupied territories

Why Bother?

It's a long way off, not easy to travel round, there are lots of political problems. People are starting to get cold feet about travelling to the Middle East. This guide tells you absolutely nothing useful about the Middle East, it is about *you*, and how you can get the most entertainment out of your trip. Because the Middle East *is* entertaining, don't worry about that. It haunts and thrills some people, some fall in love with it, others hate it on sight.

You can travel to diseased wadis and talk with incoherent madmen, you can hang out in cafés and moan along with Arab intellectuals. You can go to the strangest historical sites this side of Pluto or you can drink yourself unconscious in fake European bars. You can buy yourself embarrassing and useless artifacts of enormous size, you can go hiking, rock climbing, desert driving. You can look on the ruins of empires and despair at the old melancholy of life. You can get stoned by children in striped blankets, you can get stoned with adult males wearing John Travolta knock-offs. You can sit on camels, get bitten by camels. You can meet – well there are about two hundred million Arabs so you can almost certainly meet anyone you choose to.

What is the
Middle East?

Depends on which book you consult. The Lonely Planet guide-books exclude north Africa but include Iran and Afghanistan, and most Arabs include Sudan but exclude Israel and Turkey. There are, however, various compromises.

The Arabic-speaking world stretches from Morocco round to Yemen, with substantial Arabic-speaking minorities in Iran, Turkey and Israel. Other major languages in the region include Farsi in Iran, Kurdish in Turkey, Iran and Iraq, and Hebrew in Israel. There are lots of other languages less widely spoken – Berber, Aramaic, etc. So language doesn't give a clear picture of the Middle East. Religion then? Well, Islamic countries include Indonesia, parts of the Philippines, Pakistan and lots of other places which are clearly not in the Middle East. Also there are lots of Christians, particularly in Lebanon and Egypt and Judaism is pretty common in Israel.

Race? The Semitic stock might be one way of defining the Middle East, except for the fact that the variation over the centuries as various groups invaded or left the region means you can find any 'racial' type whatsoever from blue-eyed to jet-black African. Geography can be misleading too – Arab countries may border each other but this gives no indication of populations living in proximity. The geography of the Middle East is dominated by extensive uninhabited areas. Egypt may border Libya but the main population concentrations are separated by hundreds of miles of wasteland – the fact that they border each other is relatively irrelevant. Individual countries contain pockets of population, thus Saudis are separated geographically (and to a certain extent physically). The Asiris (just up from Yemen) live in the poorest, most populous area. Hijazis (on the Red Sea coast) are more racially mixed, sophisticated and cosmopolitan, and Nejdis, round Riyadh, are the top dogs, the puritanical ruling elite, ex-Wahabi fanatics, the boss class. A Saudi would know immediately which group any other Saudi came from, probably before the other guy opened his mouth.

Shared history? Sort of, although most of it involves invading each other, suppressing virulent minorities and forming shifty alliances. Being colonised seems to be one thing most places had in common, a shared grievance at any rate, but they were colonised by different people – British, French, Israelis, Turks and other Arabs. Politics? Anyone who believes the Middle East has a shared political mission needs his or her head examined. Arab League meetings are pathologically quarrelsome, they are nearly always boycotted by a few countries temporarily in a sulk about something and those who do turn up tend to end up shouting at each other and occasionally fighting. Economics? Hmmm. Defining the Middle East as an economic entity, there's a thought destined for the scrap heap. Rich countries have oil and indulge themselves with demented economic policies. Poor countries have lots of people and are obsessed with feeding and oppressing their populations.

For the purposes of this guide book, the Middle East will be defined on geographic grounds as Arabic-speaking countries plus Turkey and Israel. Afghanistan is excluded both linguistically and because no one in his right mind would want to visit there at the moment. Iran is excluded linguistically. The central Asian Islamic republics, the 'Stans', are excluded even though they speak Turkic languages, mostly because they have been kept out of the Middle Eastern world by the Russians and are not as yet reintegrated. Sudan is excluded as principally an African (though Islamic) country. Pakistan is excluded though it has been influential in propagating intellectual advances in Islam in the twentieth century and is the most militarily advanced of the Islamic countries. Geography rules it out; that and orientation – Pakistan's major political concern is India.

But there is a Middle East. The area is interconnected, don't be misled about that – sitting in a café in Tunisia you will see it. Watch what happens when the television shows American planes bombing Iraq, you can feel a tension in the air. A concern that an Arab country is getting its collar felt, a feeling of personal affront. It sometimes manifests itself as anger, sometimes in tears, but the feeling of being an Arab, rather than belonging to a specific country, runs very deep in the area. It is almost as if every Arab is plugged into some network, a sort of emotional tissue which binds them together. It may not be easy to define the Middle East but Arabs know what isn't the Middle East.

IMPOSSIBILITY AND THE NOVICE TRAVELLER

Some parts of the Middle East are (hopefully) not being seriously considered by travellers at the moment. One should obviously rule out Algeria, Afghanistan and Iraq unless you have a professional reason for visiting or a genuine death-wish. Some other countries, while interesting, would be a bit hair-raising for a first-time traveller to the region. There is no point scaring yourself catatonic by going to Yemen or Iran – both are excellent but are probably too tricky for an inexperienced traveller to enjoy.

The most common 'first visit' countries in the region are Turkey, Egypt and Israel. Morocco and Tunisia are popular as package destinations. For a prolonged trip, both of the north African destinations have the obvious problem of not having usable land borders – that is, Algeria and Libya are your overland options. You can actually get through Libya, but the visa situation tends to fluctuate and border tensions between Tunisia and Libya often mean that even if you do get a Libyan visa you may be turned back at the border. So for a first trip to the Middle East, what is the best bet? There you are, you've got *The Drinkers' Guide*, you've got three months, a smallish amount of money, but in truth you are a bit unsure about the whole thing. On balance Turkey is a good place to start. It seems relatively familiar, the script is Latin, which helps with road signs and menus and there is a wide variety of things to see and do.

LOST IN SPACE: PATRONISING ADVICE FOR FIRST-TIME TRAVELLERS

Well . . . here goes, might as well be prescriptive. First fly out to Turkey. It's the safest, the most westernised and there are millions of other tourists for you to talk with, but don't go to Istanbul first. Why not? Because that guide book you will be relying on for the first couple of weeks still recommends places to stay round Sultan Ahmet Square and, if there is one place in the Middle East where you are going to get ripped off before you get your bearings, it is Sultan Ahmet Square. So fly out either to Izmir or Dalaman. They are cheap to get to and getting skinned for taxi rides from the airport is about the worst that will happen. Get a three-month return if you can. These are charter airports so prices should be reasonable. So now you are in south Turkey. A lovely part of the world: beaches, ruins, all sorts of things, but you have options left for the rest of your trip, depending on how you react to a first exposure to the Middle East.

1) And it does happen.

You decide for whatever reason that you just can't stick the people, the moustaches or the sheer oddity of the area. In that case your best option is to head north for Istanbul. Easy to organise, and if you have taken a violent objection to Turks you will be a lot better prepared for dealing with Istanbul hasslers than you would have been coming to it cold. Brilliant town Istanbul and, once you've taken the edge off the unfamiliarity of the area, about as safe a city as you could imagine. Hang around there for a bit (choose a hotel in Aksaray rather than one of the Sultan Ahmet hostels). If after a week or so you really are sure you can't hack it, either go back to Izmir and get a boat to Italy, or go north from Istanbul into eastern Europe. One way or another you still get a three-month holiday, even if you end up in Poland rather than Egypt.

2) You quite like south Turkey, but are a bit unsure about what to do next. You've been hanging around for a couple of weeks and, without committing yourself, want to see a bit more.

Easy enough, carry on with Turkey for a while. It is genuinely a sub-continent in itself, and the bus services are excellent. Choose another Turkish destination and jibber-jabber your way through the travel system. Turkey is worth three months in anyone's book. I gave it three years and still hardly scratched the surface. If your confidence and interest in the area increases you can go on to at least part of three below.

3) You love Turkey, but have got itchy feet and are determined to make it to Egypt overland. Well, good for bloody you. That is what three-month holidays are for.

Head straight for Antakya (and the Syrian border), taking an excursion up into east Turkey if you are feeling macho. Or take the north Turkish loop: Ankara, Trabzon (Trebizond), Erzurum, Van and down into Syria. Check on visas for Syria in Ankara – there can be problems depending on how sulky border relations between the two are.

For all three categories your cheaply-bought three-month return ticket to Izmir or Dalaman should be of some use:

For Mr 1) If you still just hate the region after Istanbul, take the eight-hour bus journey to Izmir and if you can't organise a boat to Italy, well, fly home.

For Mr 2) You get a first-rate three months roaming round Turkey, ending up in the weird and woolly East. Come back for another two-week beach holiday in south Turkey before you go, blag up your experiences and then step on the plane. And you'll be back in the Middle East next year, I'll bet.

For Ms 3) Well, a boat out of Alexandria to Izmir means you get the return leg of your flight sorted out, but you are probably in Oman or Burkina-Faso by now going, 'Sod this university lark.'

DAY 1

For first-time travellers. Those first few hours after you arrive, you are knackered, in an airport and not really in the mood for any complicated nonsense. There are buses into town from most Arab airports, but they are never easy to find, especially if you are lugging a great heap of baggage around at three in the morning without a word of Arabic. In this case you may well end up taking a taxi into town. Get being ripped off out of your system before you start. Haggle as much as you can be bothered, team up with some other travellers and bring the cost down, but really, finding economical transport out of an Arab airport is a tricky sport and not one to undertake without some experience of the region. Wholly tourist airports like Dalaman have no public transport, but you can get a taxi to Dalaman Köy (village) which is a couple of kilometres down the road for not too outrageous a sum and there is a bus station there. Izmir has a bus but I can never be bothered remembering how to find it and most charters into Izmir arrive after it stops. You can get a normal town bus out of Istanbul airport, but it is a bitch to find. Cairo has shared taxis, but again they are well away from the main exit to the airport and you might as well finance the jackals lurking around the front door. Asking a taxi driver where the bus goes from will never get you a truthful answer. Trying to blag your way onto tourist coaches is another possibility, but it is a bit demoralising as they very rarely let you on. In short: shared taxi or bus if you can find one easily, give it ten minutes of looking around, half an hour if you are lightly loaded or have left your stuff with a travelling companion. Otherwise, taxi and curse the guy the next morning.

It is worth trying to avoid arriving late at night in big cities, but if you are going on cheap flights it's going to happen sometimes. If you touch down at three it is probably more sensible to sit around the airport til about six *then* go into town – that is, once it has started to wake up. Cairo at three in the morning is basically closed.

SAFETY IN NUMBERS

Many people believe they will be safer in places where travellers congregate; this might look logical, but these places tend to *attract* local crooks. Thus, for example, beach resorts in Sinai pull in Egyptian petty thieves from all over the country. All traveller hostels recommended in guide books are well known to locals and may well end up being magnets for the local lechers and criminals too. You may feel more at ease in the company of lots of other like-minded travellers, but there are disadvantages. You tend to meet locals from a position of being identified with a group (or type) of tourists. This means, if you like, the sins of this group are attributed to you. Thus if you are staying at a stoner hostel, if you go out, you will attract local dope-dealers like flies even if you are just out for a walk and a therapeutic pint of lager.

WHAT TO LEAVE BEHIND

If you are off on a first trip, leave forwarding addresses (poste restante, if available) for the different countries you intend to visit. Make a copy of your address book and leave that at home as well. Nothing is more certain than losing an address book when you travel. Phoning from Arab post offices is so stressful that you will almost inevitably forget your book in one of them. One way round this is to write the number you are going to phone on a scrap of paper and leave the book in your luggage, but honestly this is such a silly thing to do that you won't remember until it's too late. Make a photocopy of your passport's information pages and leave that at home, same goes for traveller's cheque numbers.

Employment

CONTRACT WORKERS

If you are thinking about signing away a couple of years to work, most probably in the Gulf countries or Saudi Arabia, this section's for you. These sorts of contracts aren't just offered to high-flying engineers, but to all sorts of teachers, builders, doctors, whatever. Think carefully before signing on the dotted line. There is a big difference between going on holiday to a moderately interesting country and spending two years stuck, bum fuck in the middle of nowhere.

Like any region, the Gulf states vary. The constants are on the surface: extreme restrictions on your personal movement, lack of alcohol, shortage of women (this is relevant both to male and female expatriates though for slightly different reasons), extremely hot and dry climates. The boom years of the Eighties are over and, where salaries for working in these countries used to be high and perks in the way of flights home and accommodation excellent, these days wages are down and conditions tend to be tighter than before. This having been said, wages are higher than in Britain for similar positions (up to 50–75 per cent higher) and jobs are available. A lot of people believe that because there is so little to do this represents a good chance to save money. That depends on your boredom threshold: if you are happy enough learning to play the flute or drooling over flat-pack furniture, you will probably be able to save quite a lot. If you start drinking heavily at Gulf prices, you will save nothing at all.

Salaries are not always paid on time. In general the Saudis try and ensure expat workers don't get their wages too far in arrears, but it does happen. Sometimes contracts are enforced to the extent of your passport being held for the duration of your contract. This is fair enough in good times, but anecdotal evidence suggests that Europeans were forced to remain in Riyadh and Bahrain during the Gulf War, bang in the middle of a war-zone.

These are some of the reasons the salaries offered are attractive. The places aren't. The best offers are the Emirates, Bahrain or Oman. Yemen is tremendous, but you don't often get offered good contracts to go there. The worst are Qatar, Kuwait, Dhahran and Riyadh. Occasionally real specialists are offered contracts in Algeria or Iraq at exceedingly high salaries – both are unacceptable for slightly different reasons. Algeria is in a lethal mess at the moment and it's open season on whitey, all foreigners are targets. Iraq, while it's a good country and the people are fine, has a very nasty government with a bad record of imprisoning foreigners more or less on a whim for years on end. Both of these countries have no functioning embassy. A no-no.

BEFORE

At the interview try and make sure of your status while in the country, and under what conditions you are entitled to junk your contract and flee the country. If it is an enforced contract (one where, if you sign up for two years that is how long you are staying, even if the whole place goes belly-up), think very carefully about it. How desperate for the money are you? Is it worth even the outside risk of being stuck in the middle of a civil war with no legal way out of the country? This particularly applies to Saudi contracts. There have been very few incidents of foreigners being deliberately targeted by anti-government groups but the likelihood is that these will become more rather than less frequent. In countries where anti-foreigner attacks occur you should make sure you are not on an enforceable contract and that in the event of things getting out of hand you are entitled to leave when *you* choose.

It is worth asking if you get a booze allowance. The odds are you won't, but it is worth a try.

DURING

'Oh *shit!*' will be your first reaction, especially if it's Qatar, but don't panic. An expatriate community exists and while it might not have people who would be your first choice of friends back home, get in there. As expat communities tend to be very small and gossipy, it's no bad idea to keep a low profile at first. Work out what the prevailing drift is before committing yourself to opinions. If you accidentally make enemies in the expat community it can take ages to get yourself rehabilitated. And you will need these folk, as a support, as a source of alcohol, as someone to talk to. For the first few weeks treat established expats like crotchety old dames you expect to get some kind of inheritance from. They tend to be deadly serious about what at first seems like nonsense. Hash-house harriers, local magazines, importing hideous furniture from Britain. Ugh, tedious stuff, but don't foul up on arrival by telling them that you think anyone who is seriously trying to collect 350 porcelain thimbles with pictures of puppies on them is off his or her head. They are bored too, and this sort of sad displacement activity becomes very dear to some of them. That and malicious gossip, so watch it.

IN TROUBLE

Trouble is almost inevitably drink-related. In Saudi local restrictions on drinking are absolute. It is simply a criminal offence to be in possession of alcohol and the punishments can be fearsome. This having been said, there is often a sort of tacit acceptance that foreigners drink. This varies, so check with the local expat community as to what the current state of play is – there are occasional clampdowns and periods of relative calm on the subject. Even during these lulls a few basic rules about drinking should be observed. First, do not offer alcohol to Muslims, and do not serve it at home when you have Muslim guests. Second, avoid being drunk in public. The authorities tend to turn a blind eye if you are getting quietly bombed at home, but pissed out of your face in public is an absolute no-no. Try not to go to work reeking of booze, especially if you are a teacher, as there will always be some pious nut-case in any class who will shop you about twenty seconds after you breathe fumes of Johnnie Walker over him. Bottle disposal should be handled sensitively as well. Dispose of booze bottles well away from your house, not in the skip at the end of your street. Wrap all bottles before disposal. These precautions are necessary even when the Saudis are being relatively tolerant. If there is a clampdown of any kind, it may be time to drink all your home-brewed hooch. The religious police are empowered to enter your home and finding booze on the premises doesn't go down well with these guys. If by some lucky freak of chance you are important enough to get an entitlement to a booze order, general rule of thumb is, be generous to other expats who don't get one and never ever in a million years sell even one bottle to a Saudi national.

WORKERS' RIGHTS

You are subject to the laws of the country you are in. Any protection you have is at the personal whim of your employer. If you are working directly for an Arab businessman, the chances of him intervening if you get caught on a drinks or drugs charge are approximately zero. You have to see his position: he cannot, however indirectly, be seen to condone drinking. European or American employers *may* interfere to the extent of getting you out of the country unpunished, but are liable to be unhappy at being put in this position and will not exactly be queuing up to re-hire you. The bigger the company you are working for, the more protection you normally have. Government employees at the embassy have a fair level of protection too.

PRISON

Hopefully not, but for Westerners this is most likely to happen for drugs charges. Expatriates can also get banged up more or less on a whim for so-called contract violations in the Gulf.

Jail terms are almost always severe and conditions wretched – in the worst cases you can be imprisoned with no clear indication of the length of your sentence. The British Embassy in theory should try to help you, but if you've broken local law there is not a great deal they can do for you. In drugs cases they may be less than helpful. So, if one of your nearest and dearest is languishing in prison in the Middle East, what should you do? A useful first stop is Prisoners Abroad, 82 Roseberry Avenue, London ECIR 4RR. Tel. 0171 833 3467.

If you are imprisoned, write to as many people as you can think of who might offer some assistance: friends, family, local MPs, anyone. Many people think of Amnesty International, but it is largely concerned with human rights and torture cases so a far more appropriate group is Release, 388 Old Street, London ECIV 9LT. Tel. 0171 729 9904. Emergency no. 0171 555 4952.

SMALL BUSINESSES. GETTING A LOT SMALLER IF YOU'RE NOT CAREFUL

Salesmen, sub-contractors and less well-connected employees are much more vulnerable to falling foul of local laws, to having their passports confiscated, or to payment of agreed money going astray. Small businesspeople can get very badly burned. As this can involve dishonoured contracts and expulsion from the country without a penny of the money you are entitled to, a bit more background reading and networking with companies which already work in the Middle East is essential. This book is too general in scope to go into all the potential pitfalls, but contact your local Chamber of Commerce for details on what constitutes a legally binding contract in the countries you intend working in. And try not to fall foul of drinking laws while negotiating a deal.

DODGY CONTRACTS

If you are bored out of your mind in a dead-end job at home and being paid peanuts, but you are not particularly well qualified, you may well run across adverts for 'Au Pairs', 'Nurses', 'Dancers' and the like in Saudi and the Gulf. The salaries look attractive and you might think: 'Well, "dancer" sounds a bit dodgy, but the other two look relatively respectable, staying with an Arab family.' Any post that involves a single woman working in a household in a Gulf country should be regarded as unsuitable. That's flat advice, though I'll spare you the grisly details. Suffice to say you are probably in a safer position if you go out as a prostitute – at least you'll have some idea of what you are letting yourself in for.

HOLIDAY JOBS

You can extend your holiday money by working as you go. The most common way of extending your stay is to do a bit of teaching in one of the numerous English schools in the Middle East. They are not normally too fussy about qualifications: having a pulse and speaking English is often sufficient to get you a temporary job. Private lessons are another possibility, though women should be careful about who they take on as students and precisely what their definition of 'learning English' includes. Teachers seeking work should drop in to the British Council. They are often short of teachers as the ones they recruit in Britain tend to go mad in imaginative manners and become unemployable. There is often work available while such teachers are dried out/bailed out/coaxed out of the cave they have gone to live in/forced at gunpoint out of the *jellaba* they insist on wearing in class.

RESIDENCE

If you want for whatever reason to overstay your visa, go carefully. It is tempting, if you are in some relaxed beach resort in Sinai and get offered a job bumming around in a café, to think, 'What the hell? I'll just hang out here, smoke my face off and not worry about visa extensions.' Even in Egypt this can land you in bad trouble when you leave. You can be fined or even jailed. It is worth getting your visa sorted out however much of a chore it appears to be.

Accommodation

WOMEN TRAVELLERS

Often a case of continual petty irritations and unwanted attention, at best. It is generally said that Arab men see European women as easy but this is an over-simplification. They are also genuinely sexually frustrated. For most Arab men (except the horrible hotel tout probably hassling you at this very moment) there is simply no sexual outlet before marriage, so even the slightest glimmer of a chance is pursued with a fervour that can seem flattering, threatening or irritating depending on your assessment of the situation. At the risk of annoying female readers and Arab men, I would say that if you end up in a room on your own with an Arab bloke for more than five minutes he might well take a grab at you and, this is the important point, may not take no for an answer. The assumption is, I'm afraid, that in agreeing to be alone with him you have already agreed to have sex with the bloke. Sad but true. Women touching men is seen as a come-on, even the sort of pat on the back of the hand many women use to emphasise points in an argument will have the guy following you for days (perhaps years), insisting that 'you have made my heart into a kebab', and 'skewered by your gaze, I am your slave'. It gets a bit wearing. Notice also in hotel shower doors little accidental looking-holes. This is pretty much standard. So unless you are really into a hidden audience while you do your pouts at the steamed-up mirror, block any of these you see.

HOW TO SAVE MONEY

If you are on a really tight budget the only useful tip is to take the second cheapest of anything on offer. *Second* cheapest? Indeed. For example, the cheapest bar in Cairo is full of hallucinating eighty-five-year-olds who have been eating shoe polish and argumentative soldiers who fight or fall asleep in the vomit-stained hole that passes for a toilet – in general, not an ambient place. In the second cheapest bar on the street (a whole penny a bottle dearer) you get marble tables, run-down 1920s decor, cool staff, virtually sane customers and a toilet you can breathe freely in.

This principle seems to work the length and breadth of the Middle East. The out-and-out cheapest is a mess and far and away the best deals are in the second cheapest category. This applies to melons, fish, souvenirs, hotels, restaurants, etc., etc. The second cheapest can still be extraordinarily cheap. For hotels it may be a jump of five pence a night from the poxed-out dormitory to the room with Art Deco furniture, clean sheets and privacy.

BAD HOTELS

Low rent hotels in the Middle East are often pretty ropy. Touts will often try and pick you up at stations and take you to hotels. Some of these on offer are not that bad and can even be reasonable deals. Good, cheap hotels are however a rarity, so if you are on a budget you have to accept some kind of compromise between the two types of cheap accommodation available. Predominantly Arab hotels sometimes double as brothels, especially in Syria and Turkey, which makes them very bad news for lone female travellers and indeed anyone. Good signs to look out for are female management or husband and wife teams, bad ones are lots of hyena-eyed young men hanging around in the front lounge. Language can be a problem in hotels not geared to tourists, but persist. Ask to be shown a couple of rooms before you decide to stay – the second one offered is often the better option.

Budget travellers often stay in entirely tourist/backpacker accommodation, as recommended in their guide books. These can be genuinely dismal places full of fat-arsed travellers sitting around moaning in groups about 'ze natives' and telling each other elaborate and tedious lies about their 'experiences'. An informal apartheid seems to have developed – these are places no Arab would consider and you too should think twice before committing yourself to these budget options. Very few people working in these hotels on the tourist circuit are locals, they tend to come from the big anonymous towns for the season. This means that the staff are less bound by local moral standards than they would be at home. If you are going to find a petty crook working in a hotel, it is likely to be in this kind of place.

Other problems of cheap places boil down to: infestation, purgatorial toilets, cold water, dirty beds (sometimes virtual ecosystems), dreadful breakfasts and unexplained extras on the bill. Which is much the same in any country in the world. Upside is cheerful staff running the joint, the perpetual promise of hot water 'tomorrow' and just the general insanities of seeing the third world at low rent.

FIVE-STAR HOTELS

You probably won't be staying in these, but the facilities are normally open to presentable-looking Westerners. Access to bars, cafés, dry cleaning, sports clubs, etc., are available at a price. If you need to change money or phone home, five-star hotels offer these services, but often at punitive rates. A note for women. You may believe you are liable to be less hassled in the Hilton bar than out in the street, but often the reverse is true. Rich Arabs can be disgracefully persistent and are not used to people saying no. Unexplained bunches of flowers arriving at your table are a typical opening gambit. Either insist they are removed, chuck them on the floor or await smoothie's arrival at your table. If you have had your entire meal ruined by unwanted attentions which you have refused, be careful about leaving on your own or the man pestering you may well follow you to carry on his invitations/protestations/generally irritating chit-chat. He may take a grab at you if you carry on refusing or suddenly switch from entreaties to volleys of unimaginative abuse. *Don't* let it start in the restaurant. Absolutely insist that the staff stop this happening, create a scene if you have to, but don't sit passively and let your holiday be ruined by unwelcome attentions. These guys are scumbags, they wouldn't dare pester an Arab woman in this way. Other Arabs *know* they are scumbags so really people are on *your* side. Mind you, if you are running short of money this sort of advance is one way of restoring the old bank balance, up to you. If you are financing your holiday this way, get cash up-front and use condoms – AIDS *is* on the go, especially in north Africa. Arab men are *very* averse to using condoms, but insist.

AIR CON

A great invention and one which budget travellers will miss out on. Trouble is (if it works) that after a boiling day, the temptation is to turn the thing up to full and chill the room down Arctic-style. Feels fabulous for a while but if you get refreshed and spring straight from the icebox back to the street, your odds of experiencing a massive coronary embolism are high. Fans, which are common in cheaper places, are probably better for you.

SLEEP

Arab hotels can be noisy late at night, and if you are a poor sleeper it might be worth considering this. The call to prayer takes a bit of getting used to. You may as well assume you'll be woken up early in the morning for the first couple of weeks of your stay at least. Some people never adjust. It doesn't in practice particularly matter, you should be able to roll over and go back to sleep again. *The Lonely Planet Guide to Jordan and Syria* (which is a really good one) suggests you take earplugs if you have trouble sleeping. It seems a bit extreme, but if you have trouble adjusting to the call to prayer, or you are in a place where there is all-night terrible music, you might wish you'd packed a pair. It seems difficult to remember to take them out in the morning, and if you want to increase your amusement value to already giggly Arabs, sitting at breakfast with a pair of earplugs in will reduce even the most stoical waiter to hysterics. Over-the-counter chemicals are an alternative.

CARDS

One thing you should always do is to get a card out of your hotel. Getting lost is no joke and even the most run-down pension has a few cards with the address of the place in Arabic. Don't rely on addresses in guide books – if you are stuck they won't get you back to home base as they are written in English. Even in small Arab towns it is quite possible to get thoroughly lost and at least with a hotel card you will get back eventually.

LAUNDRY

Quite simple, ask at your hotel, someone will do washing. Check prices in advance, they should be cheap. Unless you are genuinely impoverished don't bother doing it all yourself as once you've washed befouled socks in cold water ten times and bought soap powder, half of which you are going to leave behind when you check out, you do actually begin to realise you are losing money doing it yourself. Also I didn't know it was even legal to iron socks, so look on the bright side.

Drinking

BAR TYPES

Bars divide into two broad categories. Hotel bars and street bars.

Hotel bars are more expensive and more sophisticated (to stretch a word to its limits). These are the places to meet expatriates, pay a fortune for drink and get chatting to the local capitalist swine and their hideous offspring. Most hotels in the three-star and up bracket have these sorts of bars. In some countries (Bahrain, for example) these are the only places that serve drink. If you are running on any kind of budget at all it is essential to check prices before you start drinking. You normally pay at the end of the evening rather than per drink, so it can be a nasty shock to the system if you find out what an imported brandy actually costs after you've downed ten of them. The Middle East is a real nuisance area for solitary female drinkers as it is virtually impossible to get a drink in peace without some B-league Romeo materialising at the table. The best bet for women is probably three- rather than five-star hotel bars. The locals there are less liable to assume single woman = prostitute. Another, simpler alternative is to drink in hotels frequented by tour groups. This seems a bit defeatist though.

*   *   *

In the Arab bars you will pay between a quarter and a half as much per bottle. Cockroach-ridden true, but if you drink any amount on a regular basis these will prove to be your best bet. The people drinking in local bars tend to be more interesting than in the pseudo-European hangouts, or at least weirder and more unsightly.

Cairo, Damascus and Istanbul have the best range of these fuckholes. But most towns in non-dry countries have two or three unobtrusive bars used by local low life. Initially off putting and difficult to find, they can be detected by the betting shop analogy. If you can't see in the windows of a place that is obviously doing brisk business, odds are it's a bar and some reprobates (shame on them) are probably in there getting bombed. Words like 'Cafeteria', 'Brasserie' and 'Restaurant' are good giveaways. Should you wish to join them a couple of things are worth bearing in mind. As in the hotels, you pay at the end of the evening, so if you don't know a place, keep a tally of how many you've had as it can be a bit tricky remembering if you've had ten or eleven. Common practice seems to be to leave a tip but it's up to you. Remember you are a bit of an intrusion, so keep yourself quiet or at least don't shout any louder than the drunkest person in the bar. Keep it friendly but don't necessarily join people who ask you across. One of the commonest sub-groups in such bars are off-duty policemen and in places like Syria they may want to know your opinions on 'Our Noble Leader'. Risky even if you are sober. Also, drinking with cops sends out the wrong messages to other customers, so you end up missing out on the really good folk you often meet in such places. Such oddities as Arab loners, writers, intellectuals and out-and-out lunatics are much more fun to talk to than some bunch of policemen feeling guilty after their murky day wiring local malefactors into the mains.

Everything turns up in a bar like this eventually. If you sit there long enough you will be offered everything from bogus military secrets to dead snakes. More common are salesmen touting plastic birthday cakes or offering to test your blood pressure, beggars and shoe cleaners, all of whom are kept out of the fancier places (which is partly why you pay more, to be spared the rather gothic sight of limbless men on trolleys trying to beg from you). Up to you, but with beggars a donation seems the easiest way out (remember how much you are saving on the beer). Unless you really are a total scumbag, don't say anything along the lines of, 'I'm sorry, I am a poor man too.' You are not. Your mere presence in the country conclusively proves that, as does that beer you are drinking (impossibly expensive to locals). Be honest. Tell him to piss off if you don't like his face (or what remains of it) or give the guy some money.

One word to look out for is *jassuss*, pronounced as in the Irish Jesus (Jahsus). This means whoever said it thinks you are a spy. For some obscure reason, Arab alcoholics are convinced Israeli and American military intelligence have got nothing better to do with their manpower than to send out agents with little notebooks to write down the thoughts of a whole lot of poor and drunk Arabs. You would think any agent that sent in reports based on this sort of fact collection would be looking at unemployment pretty sharpish, but a lot of Arabs seem to believe it.

BRITISH CLUBS

You might sneer a bit at these, but if you are staying somewhere for a while it is worth trying to get guest membership, or seeing if you can drop in on open nights. These places are a bit weird, mostly done up like 1970s bars/northern working men's clubs, but if you've been travelling for some months they seem nice for a change. Also, if you are looking for work, these are the places to get into a bit of talking, a few funny handshakes and a job.

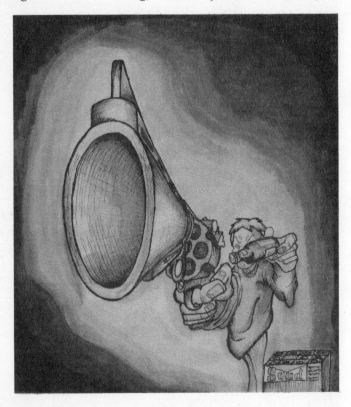

QUALITY CONTROL – AT THE BOOZE FACTORIES

Egypt

Beer-wise the only option is Stella, or the national lottery as it should be called. Sort of Russian roulette: five bottles are okay but the sixth will be a killer. Normally it is just bad sealing of the bottle – the beer doesn't froth when it's opened and smells and tastes like piss when you drink it. That is why in a good bar the beer should be opened at your table, not brought to your table with the cap off. Then the rule is, no fizz no drink. Stella Export, an allegedly premier beer, is foul and expensive. I have no idea where it might be exported to but almost certainly to countries which have subsequently severed diplomatic relations.

Turkey

Efes Pilsen is good; the only thing to watch for in tourist places is being palmed off with the crappy little 33 cl bottles at half-litre prices. Check by asking '*Büyük?*' (big) with your order. Draught beer is often watered to hell, but if not, is delicious. There is a very nice Tekel (state monopoly) beer but it is less common. Tuborg is brewed locally and is good, but you very rarely see half-litre bottles of it, which makes Efes Pilsen the one to go for. Far and away the best country for beer drinkers in the Middle East.

Jordan

Amstel is brewed locally and is fine – I've drunk a lot of it and Amstel standing. Not particularly cheap though.

Israel

Would you believe that what you drink is a political state-ment? Pro-Israelis should drink the local (very good) beer. Pro-Palestinians or those staying in east Jerusalem should drink imported beers; you won't be offered Israeli beers in Palestinian areas anyway. There isn't that much difference. Beer in Israel is good, though Israelis are not great boozers and tend (like Arabs) to be a bit disapproving of public drunkenness. There is a good range of rather uninteresting bars in Israel. This is one country in the region where you should be especially careful not to get into drunken political arguments.

Morocco

Beers are Stork and Flag. Flag is sold in insultingly small bottles (24 cl) but is the most commonly available in fancy places.

Other Countries

Where the only beer available is imported, prices can be appallingly high. This applies in Yemen, the Gulf countries and the Emirates. These places don't really sell drink openly except in a few five-star hotels, and there you are a completely captive market. Prices can get astronomical so check before you start tucking in.

If you are visiting expats and they offer you a beer, be very aware that this is a product at an extremely high premium and the easiest way to piss an expat right off is to shout 'Beer! Great!' and drink a whole lot of them. They are always in short supply so unless you are offered a second beer, switch discreetly to spirits. This particularly applies when you first arrive on a contract. You don't really appreciate how close to gold-dust beers are, and if you want to get off on the wrong foot with the expat community, being seen as a beer hound is one of the quickest ways. Invitations will soon dry up. And so will you unless you get your own booze order.

Warning

Imported drink can be *very* expensive and that can mean near fifty quid for a double brandy or ten quid for a third of a pint of Heineken. That's sterling. Extreme examples but if you are ordering imported drink especially in the Gulf make damn sure you know what it is costing you, before you start.

LOCAL SPIRITS (ESPIRIT DE CORPSE)

Not exactly a distilling centre, the Middle East, but all sorts of things are brewed up which don't kill but will knock you over. The obvious whisky for yer travelling intellectual is 'Marcel Horse' in Egypt. What is this? A la recherche du drug abuse perdu? Otherwise ersatz spirits are just that. A cheap way to get out of your face without needing a piss every twenty minutes. None will actually kill you, but most aren't too therapeutic. If they taste really horrible you can knock 'em out with Coca-Cola or Fanta. About the best of a frankly horrible bunch is Turkish gin (*cin*), which actually begins to seem drinkable before you pass out.

Raki/Arrack

These are aniseed-based spirits, which some people develop a taste for and others find consistently revolting. You will certainly end up drinking some raki in Turkey: generosity on the locals' part means you are offered it regularly. If you do like it/can stand it, people are pleased to see you drink it as it is a specifically local spirit rather than a shocking imitation of a Western one. It gives very bad hangovers, but don't they all.

Wino

Of the Turkish wines, I can recommend Büzbag because it

is so easy to remember (pronounced booze bag). There used to be a wine in east Turkey called Mal'bora — I think the producers were either in need of deep therapy or irony nuts. Turkish wine is pretty good. The most common brand is Doluca, which is perfectly palatable. The more expensive Villa Doluca didn't seem any better or worse, just twice the price. Tunisian and Moroccan stuff always tastes as if someone's left chewing gum in the bottle. Very resiny, quite drinkable though. Second bottle always tastes much better once you've got through the pain barrier. Algerian wine is better quality, but you'd need to be some dedicated wino to go to Algeria for a drink at the moment. Egyptian ones have odd names: a 'Cru de Ptolemies' does indeed taste as if a small portion of a pre-dynastic mummy has been dissolved in each bottle. Egypt has a long tradition of wine making and they aren't bad. Can't remember the names of Israeli wines, which is a good sign — there was something I called 'latrine' which I must have drunk a lot of, that may be pretty near its actual name.

Suicide Bombing

Incorrectly distilled spirits do kill on occasion, even Egyptian wine (of all things) has killed a tourist or two. There is no advice here: if you are drinking illicitly distilled booze you take your chances. You are safe enough if the guy has been doing it for a while, if only because poisoning your entire customer base is uneconomic. If the person making it has been paying attention you won't come to any harm. I've drunk spirits distilled by Yemenis and if there is one people who genuinely know fuck-all about distilling it's Yemenis. Drink it if you can get it would be about the rule of thumb. Two years sober in Qatar is much more likely to kill you than playing Russian roulette with your liver.

Food

THEY CALL ME MR PITTA FUUL

That is bread and beans, the fuel of the Middle East. These two might make up the bulk of an Arab's daily diet for every day but one a month. Bread is always available fresh anywhere in the Middle East and is uniformly delicious. *Fuul* is the broad bean, ground into a paste with the colour, smell, texture and occasionally taste of . . . (well see if you come up with the same word). Other cheapies are *felafel* – deep-fried chickpeas and coriander. What else do poorish Arabs eat? Salad, vegetables and fruit are part of everyone's diet, however poor. Yoghurt is one 'luxury' Arabs are reluctant to do without. It's not a starvation diet, but it's not very varied either.

In the home meat is rarely eaten, except by rich Arabs or at celebrations. Chicken is the exception – most poor households have a couple of chickens wandering about in the yard. However, if Arabs have guests they *will* put meat on the table, even if they can't really afford it. If you want to spare your host financial embarrassment, check in the vegetarian section of this book (p.43), the Arabic phrase there should stop him killing anything for your dinner. As for you, if invited it's no bad thing to take something along. The problem is, it can be quite difficult to gauge whether your host is impoverished or not. Rather too many guide books suggest taking along a kilo of meat. This is fine if the guy is a street sweeper, but if you are visiting a middle-class Egyptian family, it would be an embarrassing mistake. The safest is to take along some kind of cake or sticky sweet – this is socially okay with a well-off family and for a poor one it is a genuine treat.

CHEAP THRILLS

Cheap 'street eats' are fine if a bit monotonous eventually. The basic staples are, again, *fuul* and *felafel*. Macaroni or rice with sauce is also a cheap option. One step up from these are the greasy spoon dishes, metal pots of lukewarm stuff, with cold rice. These can vary from the disgusting to the filling, but in general are not wildly inspiring. Eating meat tends to be more expensive. Chicken is the cheapest meat. Chickens are roasted in a glass-fronted case outside the restaurant and you either order one or a half, with whatever else they have in stock – salad and yoghurt is normally the minimum. Kebabs, of course, vary from the okay to the excellent if the meat has been well marinaded and the grilling done freshly. What we call doner kebab is called *schwarma* in the Middle East and is widely available; some travellers swear blind that these cause food poisoning, they generally do nothing of the kind. If you want to be double-careful, buy from a place which is doing a brisk local trade. The seasoned, ground meat kebabs are good too. Watch out for grilled internal organs, which occasionally turn up masquerading as muscle meat. Locally manufactured pizzas are another cheap- to mid-priced option. Called *pide* in Turkey and pizza elsewhere, they are as much a Middle Eastern food as any other.

You can of course get wretched food all over the place.

Three-star hotel meals are as grim and unimaginative as they are anywhere in the world. As an obvious rule of thumb any place where everyone eating is European and everyone serving is tarted up in fezzes and curly-toed slippers is going to be indifferent at best. Don't be shy of packed places with nothing written in English. Follow the locals. I mean, Arabs aren't lunatics, if they are eating Egyptian food in an Egyptian restaurant it seems a bit unlikely that they are deliberately paying to poison themselves with the sort of things they could easily cook at home. Whatever most people in a cheap restaurant are eating is likely to be a) fresh, b) not fatal, c) a laugh. Arabs are exceptionally kind and helpful to lost-looking foreigners. If you can't read the menu either point at what you fancy or (more common) wait for someone who speaks a bit of English to abandon his own meal to help you decide.

EXPENSIVE EATS

You can pay more than most Arabs could and get a temporary escape from Arab food in every capital city in the Middle East. Chinese restaurants are often good and there are quite a few of them. You may feel it's a bit odd going to a Chinese restaurant in, say, Jordan, but when the thought of another kebab is making you twitchy, it is not a bad idea. Less successful are the fake European restaurants which go in for the ·presentation but less often come with anything memorably edible and some-times come up with something memorably unkeepdownable. The French influence can be seen in the ill manners of the waiters, the steepness of the prices and the meanness of the portions. Almost indistinguishable from France really. If you've been on a largely vegetarian/Middle Eastern diet for a couple of weeks, breaking your routine with a steak plays merry hell with your digestion. For good expensive Arab food it is worth checking to see if there are any Lebanese-run restaurants. They tend to go in for some of the best Middle Eastern cookery and, while not the cheapest in town, you stand a good chance of a really splendid eat. Other up-market Arab food can be found in fish restaurants. If a town is on the coast, odds are you can get first-rate fish and all the trimmings without crippling your budget.

You can get burgers and fast food all over at middling prices. The nastiest burger joints are the Kentucky Fried Chicken outlets which are littered round the Middle East. These have been franchised to some guild of food poisoners and are much more likely to blow out your lower intestine than the shittiest-looking Arab restaurant.

TAP TIPS

Don't get over-neurotic about tap water − in general it is drinkable, but better not to drink too much of it. From a traveller's point of view though, it should definitely be second choice. Take your own bottled water to restaurants (where it is available, it is a bit pricey). Ice cubes are *always* made from tap water; this seems pretty obvious, but many tourists relax somewhere like the Hilton and unwittingly assume that somehow that iced drink is made with mineral water ice cubes. This is just idiotic, no hotel in the world is going to do this. If you are avoiding tap water, ironically enough it will be five-star places that catch you out; cheaper places don't use ice, they freeze the drinks, bottle and all, which is a lot safer from your point of view.

SERVICE WITH A SMILE AND SOMETIMES A SLITHER

There is some rule in Egypt that staff must both outnumber customers and suffer from dualistic impulses. They are attentive to your every need, to the point of being rather intimidating when a hand pops up from under the table to light your cigarette. It can become infuriating if you get a plate-shifter – a minor neurotic sub-group but very strikable. This is a man who lurks round your table for the duration of your meal, moving each of your plates fractionally when he thinks you are not watching that particular one. On another day the numerous staff will get all introverted and hang around in the back of the restaurant contemplating the void, and cannot by any stratagem be coerced into taking the slightest interest in customers. Eating out is mostly pretty chummy, with guys talking to you and offering you food (or in Yemen eating yours, or indeed snatching it and running off down the street with it if they think you don't want it, or it matches their suit, or it's Thursday). In general terms packed places are the best bet: the waiters don't have time to indulge themselves with the service or to settle into millennial gloom.

Remember the 'second cheapest' rule if confronted by a street of seemingly identical chicken restaurants. Bad signs are complete emptiness, anything dead lying under the table, people coming out of the restaurant trying to drag you in (only in touristy areas) or people sleeping on the premises.

CHEAPSKATES

Pathologically mean backpackers are a bore. They will only take the cheapest of everything. They will embarrass you by haggling over the most minuscule sums of money. So big deal, you save three pence a night by sleeping in the urinal of your hotel? Well done Klaus. Thankfully the real tight wads tend to get invalided out of the proceedings on a fairly regular basis, as saving a penny by eating in the shitbox restaurant with the dead cats under the tables is what they call a short-term investment. These meanies always complain bitterly about toilets as well, most likely because they end up spending forty per cent of their holidays in them.

BRAINS TRUST

For some reason lamb's brain is a common bar snack in parts of the Middle East. Personally I don't even like sharing a table with something that looks like an out-take from *Invasion of the Bodysnatchers*. The only European I knew who ate one of these, took one spoonful and passed dead away off her stool. They may be edible. Turks are fans.

THE SOUP OF DEATH

Key word here is the Turkish dish *işkembe*. Now normally when something revolting is brought to the table it is easy enough to spot, but this innocuous and quite tasty soup is fine until you plumb the bottom of the bowl and come up with a bit of stomach or a string of alveoli. If you are averse to innards

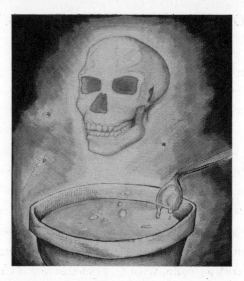

and find this junk in the bottom of your plate and have a hangover . . .

DAY TO DAY

In general terms, apart from one burst of the runs when you first arrive in the Middle East, you won't get anything serious from any cheap eaterie that is doing a brisk trade. Wash your hands before and after eating – there is always some water available. If you are expected to eat with your hands, use the right hand only.

Using the left hand is to be avoided when shaking hands or eating in public – toilet paper hasn't really caught on in the Middle East and the left hand is used in its place. As eating is often from communal dishes, using the left hand can be seen as pretty squalid table manners.

HOW TO BRAISE AN OX OR AT THE BUTCHER'S (NOT ONE FOR VEGETARIANS)

Buying beef can be fairly gothic, with live cattle being marked out with felt pens in little stone cubicles. Naive old me didn't work out what was going to happen next even when Mr Monster turned up with his neolithic axe. Yes you've guessed it, dismantle still living cow along felt pen lines, blurggh. Buying lamb was a bit of a problem as well. I asked the butcher at the market about this and he took me to a pen full of sheep and said, 'Which would you like?' The sheep are just standing there going, 'Meh meh' and subtly indicating each other. So I picked one (well, I was hungry) and the bum wouldn't even kill it for me. He gave me a bit of string to take it home on. What am *I* expected to do? Chase it up to the roof and kick it off? Vegetarianism or servants is the only answer for long-term Middle East residents.

EVERYTHING IS UNAVAILABLE

Guide books tend to give a mouthwatering list of foods which are served only in family houses or at festivals or in really flash Arab restaurants. Even in big towns limited menus are the rule. Most Arabs eat at home, so restaurants can be rare in out-of-the-way places. The traveller can easily end up having to depend on local food handouts or being restricted to the hotel staff's leftovers. Villages, unless they are having some kind of festival, will not have much variety of food in any restaurants they might have. The odds are it will just be *fuul*, *felafel* and rice, maybe *schwarma* or chicken, if you're lucky.

VEGETARIANS

Most guide books to the Middle East do vegetarians a great disservice. Normally the Arabic for vegetarian is given as either *bidoon lahm* or *ana la akul laham*. *Neither* of these offers the slightest guarantee that you will receive a meat-free dish. They can be taken to mean, respectively, 'remove meat' or 'I am not eating meat' (at this moment). The problem is that vegetarianism does not ring any bells in the Middle East: if you have money you eat meat, simple as that. It is worth having a proper explanation of your objection to eating meat for two reasons. Firstly, what looks like a bowl of vegetables can just be a meat dish with the most obvious chunks fished out. This leads vegetarians to utter grief when they find an unobtrusive hoof lurking at the bottom of the bowl. Secondly, if you are invited to an Arab's house he will, however poor, endeavour to put meat on the table, happily wrecking the family budget to give you a good impression. Save him some money, alert him well in advance. The handy, wallet-sized, cut-out-and-keep card below establishes without invoking religion that eating meat is something you just do not do, in any circumstances.

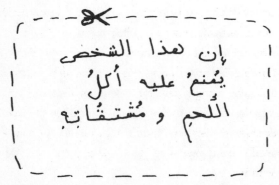

Love or Sex?

WHITE WOMAN: COME WITH ME

You will undeniably get a lot of attention when you travel in the Middle East. What you do about it is up to you. Comments on the street can be more or less ignored – try and look purposeful if you are walking around. Anyone who takes a grab at you requires more action: either shout at him or hit him hard on the nose. In general more respectable Arabs will chase the guy off – it would be unthinkable that any local woman would be treated in this way so why should you be? If you are drinking on your own, one suggestion is to buy two drinks, sit one at the other end of the table and insist you are waiting for someone and so Romeo is not welcome to slither into the seat opposite. More practical would be to get an individual waiter in a hotel bar on your side – he will then be protective and supportive in chasing off unwanted additives to your table. This is not recommended in a hotel you are actually staying in as it is by no means uncommon for your waiter 'friend' to materialise at your bedside at three in the morning intent on cementing the friendship. Unwanted attention can be a nightmare for single female travellers (you meet them occasionally in hotel bars spitting with fury after some particularly distasteful piece of sexual harassment), but you generally do get used to it and find your own ways of dealing with it.

ARAB BOYFRIENDS

Well, go with the flow. May seem like a good idea but you will receive an extremely strange letter three months later proposing marriage in mangled English. Arab boyfriends are exceptionally attentive, get preposterously jealous and value you more for your availability than any other feature you may believe you possess. Do bring your own condoms as AIDS is on the go, in north Africa particularly. Fidelity is a problem with Arab boyfriends and your status is pretty much fixed at the second-class-citizen level. This will not be a great problem if you resume your relationship in Britain, but be *extremely careful* of marrying and going to the Middle East. Be very clearly aware that your legal status married to an Arab man living in the Middle East is little above that of chattel, and while you may well be lucky with your husband, if things go sour you can forget custody of any kids and may be lucky to get out of the country.

For women, relationships with Arab men are easy to organise (impossible to avoid if you are travelling on your own?). Pick your man with care, don't flirt with anything that makes your skin crawl and remember in effect you've got the choice of however many million men there are in the country so don't just settle for the first waiter who hits on you.

ARAB GIRLFRIENDS

This means marriage or the threat of imminent death from a vast extended family. Marriage involves conversion to Islam, which means among other things taking on an Islamic name. Not put off yet? Well go ahead, marry her. Arab women can be ferociously money-orientated though. The beautiful simple girl you meet might get Imelda Marcos syndrome once her cash-flow is sorted out (this means your bank balance) and start to buy startlingly vile clothes in enormous quantities. Arab women do find European men attractive, but mostly because anything which offers a bit of freedom looks relatively good. Sexual inequality means that relationships with Arab women mostly boil down to outrageous flirting sessions, with little prospect of consummation as every Arab man will do his damnedest to make sure you never get more than thirty seconds alone together. A sexual relationship needs to be organised with the sort of meticulous planning and evasionary techniques of a military campaign. It's sort of a laugh, but make sure you don't get caught, the consequences for her could be disastrous, even fatal. This is a serious point, and one which any responsible man should think very carefully about. If you are having a sexual relationship with an Arab woman and her family find out, she is in deep trouble. It is not acceptable for you just to sneak off to the nearest airport; the woman you leave behind is really in the shit. She is held to have brought shame on the family, and will be punished. This can, in loopadoolly countries, include her family killing her. So it's not a joke. If you really love her you should start making plans from whichever day you realise this to get her out of the country at short notice.

If you just fancy a quickie, don't start the relationship, just head for the nearest tourist hotel and chat up that perfectly nice Danish woman who is in a spitting rage after another afternoon of harassment. She might be pleased to meet you.

Yemen – 'The Land that Time Forgot'

Yemen is experiencing a modest colour-supplement-fuelled tourist boom. Ever-effusive copywriters have excelled themselves in the packaging of a relatively unfamiliar new country. 'Mediaeval' is the key word: the experience is held to be authentic, Ye Olde Arabia advertised as 'The Land of Queen Sheba', 'The Land that Time Forgot'. Yemen is being sold as a wonderland cum Disneyland. Facts are much trickier to come by. I was still wrestling with trowel loads of this romantic drivel as I sat on the plane to Sana'a. I asked the sophisticated-looking Arab in the next seat if he was from Yemen. He wasn't, he said, but was working there.

'Yemen is hell,' he confided. 'They are drug-taking savages. Not Arabs. Very dangerous place. I am always happy to get home alive.'

'Where are you from?'

'Beirut.'

Hardly reassured, I sat tight as we touched down; three bounces, at Sana'a airport.

The capital, Sana'a (and Yemen as a whole), is working overtime to catch up with the rest of the world. Isolated under a backward-looking theocracy, Yemen was first opened to outside influences in 1962 and, because of a protracted series of civil wars, in effect started from scratch in the late Seventies. This is most immediately apparent in Sana'a where rapid modernisation – streets packed with locally bowdlerised Toyotas – exists side by side with possibly the most completely untouched old city in the world, which is now being maintained and restored with 250 million dollars of UNESCO's money. Sana'a's city centre is a tangled sinister maze, crowds packed in narrow twisting canyons of streets. Almost anything can be bought there and almost all of it is imported – Russian matches, Indian razor blades, Chinese flip-flops – even 'local' products are often imported: the characteristic South Arabian curved dagger, the *jambiya*, is Made in Taiwan and ethnic water pipes come from India.

Most Yemenis live outside the main cities, over half of them in villages of less than five hundred people, working the fertile patches of this harsh, mountainous country. Water from the *wadi* floors irrigate the steep terraced hillsides. Topographically, Yemen is a country split into different levels as if dirty dinner plates from three or more meals had been stacked one on top of the other. The land sweeps down from high infertile peaks and plateaus through a rich band of agricultural land to sea level, with a baking sub-tropical strip running parallel to the Red Sea. In the east, Yemen tails off into low-lying sandy desert, eventually reaching the Indian Ocean and the port of Aden. Most of my trips round the country were in shared taxis – an opportunity to meet normally reticent Yemenis at very close quarters. Yemenis are reluctant to invite strangers into their fortress-like homes but in a communal taxi enforced proximity and the prevailing holiday air of travellers returning to their home villages makes for fast friendships. The taxis stop frequently at seemingly desolate spots; your neighbour stretches, picks up a knotted bundle and disappears down some barely visible track to a lower outcrop on which, scarcely distinguishable from the surrounding rock, a tiny village can be seen. If you are lucky you may be invited into houses or to see a farmer's smallholding. Even in the semi-desert eastern provinces I was shown mangoes, peppers, cotton, onions, bananas and of course *qat* all flourishing in irrigated pockets where all around is bleached out, inhospitable desert.

Yemen is an agricultural country and most of the money is in the land. The staple, or at least principal crop is *qat* and Yemen revolves around the social chewing of its mildly euphoric leaves. As you travel you are continually offered little fresh smelling bundles of leaves by Yemenis with bulging cheeks and green-stained teeth. All for fitting in with local habits, particularly narcotic ones, I stripped my first few sprigs and, with expert guidance, started to chew. The trick is to store the pulp in your cheek without swallowing the leaves, taking in only the acrid juice produced. Even if the thought of appearing with obvious vegetable matter about your person is distasteful, you will give in eventually. The effects, while not marked, add noticeably to the comfort of your journey. The seat seems to expand and Yemen ceases to seem such an alien mishmash. The Japanese car rolls along the German roads, through a mountainous landscape where vultures glide below you.

Yemenis say they dream and plan with *qat* but that their fancies disappear the next morning. The leaves stored in my cheek gradually become a bitter irritant, and the journey begins to oppress as skinny elbows dig into my cramped sides. Yemenis hawk and spit, blithely lighting up cigarettes in concert at every petrol station. I ache to expel the painful lump of leaves from my mouth, sullenly counting the remaining kilometres to my destination. Unused to tourists, village Yemenis can be shy or, in the case of children, curious and persistent. I was followed by a howling chorus: 'Egyptian?', 'Korean?' and even, in out-of-the-way places, 'Roman?'. As the stones rattle around you, the plan may be to repeat to yourself that they are just interested in foreigners. Otherwise, spin quickly and throttle the first child you can catch.

Towards the end of my stay the BBC World Service announced, of all biblical disasters, that a plague of locusts was about to descend on Yemen. Gloomy visions of agricultural disaster were put to rest as the announcer, with a sly eye on the perverse Yemeni nature, continued: 'Locusts which have destroyed the crops in Sudan, eaten everything that grows in Ethiopia, have now come to Yemen – where they will all be eaten.'

And so it came to pass. Wheelbarrow loads of browny-pink roasted locusts were consumed with a revolting enthusiasm. As I left for the airport the taxi driver informed me that they were considered a great delicacy. And what's more they never touched the *qat* crops.

So I left Yemen to its oven-baked natural disaster and national leaf, about as confused as when I had first arrived. When my photos were returned I gave up: cutesy chocolate-box mediaeval to the last frame. No description does the place justice – Yemen remains its own country, resolutely indifferent to the opinion of the outside world.

A Potted History
of the Middle East

AD 600

The remains of the Roman Empire – the Byzantine Empire – had been weakened both by war and by barbarian incursions from Central Asia. The tribal people in Arabia had previously been no more than an irritant; one of those places which nobody can be bothered colonising, like Scotland, you build up your defences to keep the local gibberwits out and forget about them. But out in the dunes big things were happening. Monotheistic religion had been revealed to Mohammed and proved overwhelmingly popular, beating the worship of large black stones into a cocked hat. This, combined with overpopulation and a generalised desire to get out of the desert, led to the first Islamic conquests. The Arabs set off to conquer the world. At which they proved to be excellent. This next century or so was impressive, leaving the Byzantine Empire doing a Butch Cassidy and the Sundance Kid: 'Who are these guys?' They lost even more territory, corresponding more or less to modern Egypt, Syria, Jordan and Palestine. The Byzantine Empire was always vulnerable to outside pressure. In this case the weak point was Palestine – once the Arabs reached the Mediterranean, the Byzantines were cut off from their north African provinces, which fell like ninepins to the invading armies. The central core of the empire was under attack too. Even Constantinople was besieged in 717, but the rump of the empire held on, just.

By about 750 the Arab Moslems had expanded right through north Africa (though the Berber tribes of Morocco and Algeria were putting up a tough resistance), up into Spain, and were fighting land battles in the south of France against Charlemagne. To the east the expansion was equally impressive. The Persian Empire had fallen as early as 650 and some fifty years later Samarkand and the Punjab were also under Arab control.

The Zenith of Arab Power

While Europe was still at the mud-hut stage of civilisation, the Arabs were building a glorious empire – the capital shifted from Damascus to Baghdad, the dynasty from Ummayyed to Abbasid, but there was little doubt that this was the most powerful empire around. Culturally it thrived, intellectually advances were being made that would take Europe 500 years to catch up on, militarily it was pretty powerful, but there is always going to be a weakness in any empire and in the Arab case it turned out to be administrative. Blame communications, personal ambitions or the like, but the fact remains that provincial governors became too powerful and either ran their parts of the empire as private 'countries' or revolted and tried to take over the whole empire.

Empires never last. Either internal strife leads to a break-up or external enemies break in. When the two are combined it is fatal.

Nomadic Empires

Obviously nomadic empires aren't famous for leaving ruins, so it is easy to underestimate their size and influence. Nomadic empires do however form a key theme of mediaeval history. The general plot runs as follows. Nomadic groupings in either Central Asia or the Arabian peninsula form an alliance. They sit around in furs (or rags) wondering what the meaning of it all is, and if felt tents, small horses and disgusting food constitutes a tolerable lifestyle. The answer is, inevitably, no. So logically enough the decision is taken to go for sun, sea, gold and babes. The defending Mediterranean empire having spent a lot of time on booze and babes get knocked over fairly quickly. The Nomads become 'assimilated' and settle down to counting the gold and changing their clothes from rags to silk and generally having a whale of a time.

Meanwhile in the steppes of Central Asia overpopulation looms again. The tribal elders form an alliance to discuss whether they are satisfied with felt tents, greasy offal sandwiches and religious rites too disgusting and silly to persist with. The answer is inevitably NO! And so it all goes on . . .

1100

The Empire Strikes Back. By 1100, the Caliph was still in Baghdad, but the empire was starting to crumble. Sub-dynasties which paid very little attention or money to the Caliph had long been established in Spain, north Africa, Yemen and Egypt. The outside world was looking more hostile too. The Arabs had been coasting and it was going to really cost them dear . . . not just once but again and again.

Out there in the north and west were a lot of real losers, mediaeval shell-suit wearers tooling up for a bit of millennial biffing. Europe had been doing overpopulation and squalor and had the bright idea of exporting these wonderful assets. We call this visitation the Crusades. The Byzantine Empire was still more or less hanging on and hoped that these Crusader Christians might piss off out of the remains of their nice empire, whop a few Arabs and more importantly stop picking fights on their territories. The Crusaders responded by getting wiped out, capturing bits of the Byzantine Empire, then sacked the whole thing in a fit of joie de cretinism in 1204. This was of no great interest to the Arabs except to the local landowners in Syria and Palestine who had a whole lot of sun-block lager louts building castles, shagging daughters and generally causing a nuisance on the beaches. The Crusaders were little more than a large group of football hooligans who set up a whole lot of mini-states and were shouting, 'Here we go!' from the walls while the Arabs were doing much more interesting things – like having civil wars.

The Arab world was beginning to fragment along what we would now recognise as national lines. Being incapable of exerting their united powers meant that the Arab world was increasingly vulnerable to invasions. The Christians were beginning to regain a toe-hold in Spain, and the fact that the Crusader states managed to get themselves established at all is more a testament to Arab division than to European strength. The strictly 'Arab' identity of the empire was being eroded by regular incursions of Nomads who took over bits of the old empire. It looked like a non-Arab people would one day take over control of the Arab lands. The final blow came from the east when Baghdad was sacked in 1258 by Hulugu Khan. The Mongol general had the last Caliph kicked to death and, according to contemporary accounts, heaped 800,000 corpses in the streets. Central Asia kept throwing up ever more annoying bunches of aggressive nomads – the enchanting Mongols blasted everything they could get hold of, made it as far as Syria and for a while it looked as if they might break into Egypt. They were swiftly followed by the Turks (short snappy name), who went down a storm, sort of. They came tearing into what remained of the Arab world, picked up the last bits of the Byzantine Empire and galloped up through the Balkans. They got as far as Vienna, then calmed down a bit, thought about it, and started to run their empire from Istanbul. As well as being pretty hot news on the battlefield, they were excellent administrators, and didn't for a long time make the mistake of allowing too much provincial autonomy. It happened eventually, of course, and the Turks in turn got sloppy. They chilled out and after a while made the tactical error of changing their names to 'Ottomans'. The Arabs looked upon this new name and found it silly, which meant they were allowed to revolt again.

1750

Ruled from Istanbul, the Arab world became increasingly difficult to control. The Turkish elite spoke a different language and Istanbul was simply too near the edge of the Arab world to exercise control. This wasn't helped by the meteoric rise of the West and the increasingly obvious fact that these were pretty damn horrible people and their nasty little local wars were beginning to spill over into the Middle East. The warning signals were there.

1800

At first the Arabs, Persians and Turks were pretty uninterested in the Europeans. Like the Chinese they thought, 'Who are these fuckheads in the weird clothes?' There was some mild admiration for clocks and pen-knives, but no real expectation that one horrible day this shower would appear on the doorstep, all guns blazing, and generally end up having as much nuisance value as the Mongols or the Huns. As usual, the trouble kicked off in Egypt.

Egypt had more or less sunk into complicated dynastic torpor. Napoleon decided to intervene – not that he had anything against Egypt, it was just an attempt to disrupt British communications with India. The French won their last land battle there against the assembled striped pyjamas and rusty swords of the Mameluke armies in the Battle of the Pyramids, 1798. It was the first time Europe had intervened militarily in the Middle East since the Crusades, but it wasn't going to be the last, not by a long chalk. After this Egypt was open to the French who wisely decided against taking on this mare's nest of idiocy and gave it back to the nominal control of the Turks. Egypt then revolted (not just the Turks but itself as well). Mohammed Ali punched his way into the headlines, effectively ruling Egypt outwith Turkish control. Which, it just shows you, proved to be temporarily quite rich. The British discovered washing and cotton, so Egyptian cotton became the big commodity play of the 1850s. The new rulers in Egypt discovered the art of borrowing far too much money, and attempted a sort of overnight modernisation programme which, while it got some way along the road, didn't do much for the old balance books. The British then invented repossession. Though if the Egyptians had realised debt collection was quite so closely related to baseball-bat diplomacy they would probably have borrowed from someone else. The British got all superior and decided, 'Independent other countries, no thanks,' and picked up the Egypt franchise. Then they discovered international law, which proved it was illegal to take Egypt away from them and that they were pretty hot shit and all that. Colonialism sometimes looks rather strange translated into English.

By this stage the Ottoman Empire was being called 'the sick man of Europe', which in effect meant that it was okay to pick up as many Arab countries as were lying about – the Turks presumably being so sick they wouldn't mind and, as the Arabs could be whacked around on the battlefield, that meant it was okay to take over their countries. The Europeans moved in – bad landlords the Arabs reckoned.

1900

Anyway the Germans all woke up from their swinish slumber and went, 'What happened to the world? Are there any bits left we can have?' They were given a lucky bag of assorted pest holes but got bored playing around in them and so biffed the shit out of Europe twice in the hope of getting more real estate. In fact they ended up cut into three strips and generally wearing the 'Kick me I'm the bad guy' reputation. Very sensibly the Arabs used all these European wars as an opportunity to get rid of the colonising powers, and set up as independent countries. Which we then proceeded to interfere in, destabilise and generally play silly buggers with until they got really sick of us.

Post-war History

After the Second World War everyone was exhausted, including the European powers operating in the Middle East. America had gained a lot of influence over Britain and France and was looking to extend its economic influence in the Middle East. This they thought would best be achieved by levering Britain out of oil concessions in the Gulf. More generally the Americans tended to back any move for independence by Arab countries and indeed put indirect pressure on the colonising power to leave. The big new post-war variable in the Middle East was American meddling.

Britain had already promised Egypt full independence, but was intent on keeping control of the Suez Canal. The other bits of real estate that the British were responsible for were: Iraq, which was clearly ready for independence, the two mandated territories Palestine and Transjordan, which Britain was dying to get rid of, and South Yemen, or more accurately Aden, and whichever local hopheads were currently taking bribes. All the Emirates and Kuwait were under British control too. Post-war the immediate policy was to get rid of as many overseas commitments as possible – Britain was in effect bankrupt and colonies had stopped showing much of a profit. This retreat was planned in two stages . . . The most urgent was to get rid of Palestine and Transjordan as they had become ungovernable. The fact was the British were very much to blame for the mess in Palestine but were reluctant to accept their responsibilities. The Jews were establishing a *de facto* state, everyone was squabbling like mad and the Brits wanted to get this one dumped fast. They got out by referring the problem to the UN in 1947. Britain then pulled out its troops in mid-1948 and Ben-Gurion declared the state of Israel the next day.

Israel came into existence in 1948 and was immediately subject to one of the most incompetent invasions ever staged. In theory every Arab country was in on this but some of them seem basically to have missed Israel altogether and invaded each other. It was a shambles. The Palestinians ran for it, setting up in temporary refugee camps (or so they thought) inside Jordan and the Gaza Strip. They are still there today, but inside what is now 'greater' Israel, which as you can imagine pisses them off more than somewhat.

THE 1950s

A glory era for the Arabs. Smiting the imperialist devils, lots of conferences, nationalism, assassinating kings, that sort of thing.

Britain spent a lot of time in the Fifties propping up unpopular kings and governments who were variously strangled, mangled or exiled by nationalist governments. First Egypt went down as King Farouk sailed off into the sunset in 1952 taking 204 pieces of luggage with him. Obviously he wasn't just planning a weekend trip. Britain was left with a new and increasingly unfriendly regime to deal with. The main players were Gamal Abdel Nasser, the Egyptian leader who became president after the 1952 coup d'état, and the British, the declining imperialist devils.

British policy in Egypt was to up sticks more or less overnight, maybe hanging on to a few strategic points and the Suez Canal zone. The independent Egyptians nationalised the Suez Canal Company out of spite when the British and Americans refused to put up the money for the Aswan Dam. At which point Britain, France and Israel came up with a fantastically insane plan: to invade Egypt and ... recolonise it? Partition it? Turn it into a theme park? The planning wasn't that detailed. They forgot to mention this idiotic scheme to the Americans, who took a fit and refused to have anything to do with it. The Soviets weren't too happy either. The British reconsidered – not only was the project an expensive mess, it could blow the lid off the whole Middle East. So Britain bottled it and backed down and it was a triumph of Arab power, or so Nasser insisted. Really it was just a British cock-up. Britain's other royal friends were in Iraq and, after the shambles in Egypt, Britain reckoned it could hold the line there. Wrong again. Iraq went belly-up in 1958 and this time the king didn't make it to his yacht. He and his government were bloodily assassinated. King Hussein in Jordan reacted to being a British client king with a bit more style. He carried out a coup d'état *against* his own nationalist government and kicked out his British advisors. King Hussein is just one of the survivors, he's still there today.

The French disengagement from the Middle East was handled more eccentrically. Syria was arbitrarily divided into Syria (the crap bit) and Lebanon, which the French created as a state which would have a numerical balance between Christians and Moslems, presumably so that when they did have a civil war it would go on for a bloody long time as the sides were so evenly matched. In north Africa they tried a different plan. By the early Fifties it was clear that they were no longer welcome, violence was becoming endemic, so Morocco and Tunisia were given independence and the Algerians were told that they were French. Understandably this didn't go down too well, civil war broke out and a long and bloody struggle for independence was fought costing, at most estimates, a million Algerian lives. The French behaved brutally in the extreme and the latter stages of the war involved some shameful military practices. Algeria got the independence it deserved in 1962.

THE 1960s

After all the excitement of independence and Arab Nationalism, things began to slide. Egypt had united with Syria in a fit of brotherhood which turned sour so rapidly that it nearly led to war, particularly after the Syrians commented that this was the first time a white country had been colonised by a black one. Egypt invaded Yemen instead and, like everyone who has meddled in the internal affairs of Yemen, got bogged down, slaughtered and thoroughly sick of the pathologically quarrelsome and dangerous Yemenis. The Saudis didn't like this development one little bit (even in the Sixties Saudi Arabia was dead against nationalist revolutions on its doorstep), so they backed the Yemeni royalists and a long-drawn-out civil war ensued. Saudi, alarmed by Nasser's popularity and the revolutions going on around the Arab world, was edging increasingly into the centre of Arab politics. By the mid-Sixties the Arabs had got sick of invading each other and forming worthless alliances so the reckoning was to 'invade Israel again'. While they were thinking about this and cranking up the rhetoric, Israel invaded virtually the entire Middle East.

The Six Day War

In 1967 Israel took on the Middle East and, whichever way you try and dress it up, cuffed them. The effects were traumatic on the Arabs; a deep sense of inferiority and self-disgust took root. The Palestinians were forced out of what remained of their lands, Syria lost the Golan Heights, Egypt the Sinai desert. Jordan lost the West Bank and crucially Jerusalem. In terms of disasters this was the one that most shaped the Middle East we see today. The

UN brokered a cease-fire as much out of pity as anything else as it looked like any further continuation of the war was going to lead to the Israelis capturing the whole Middle East from Cairo to Damascus.

This war and the one in Yemen undermined Egypt's assumption of the leadership of the Arab world, and the Saudis, under the astute King Faisal, reluctantly edged towards this nominal role. The Saudis were anti all sorts of things, but were particularly keen anti-Russians and the thought of Soviet satellite states surrounding them (principally Syria, Egypt and Iraq) motivated the Saudis into two linked policies which were to have long-term and arguably disastrous effects. First was to forge stronger links with America and second was to dole out money to relatively friendly Arab states. The sight of all the kings of the region going down like ninepins in the 1950s had left a deep impression on the Saudi royal family.

Israel spent the rest of the Sixties strutting. No winner in the Middle East can resist making the opposition eat boiled crow.

THE 1970s

Egypt tried another war against Israel – the Yom Kippur or Ramadan offensive in 1973. This was more a draw than a calamity, so the Egyptians salvaged some pride. In an attempt to exert some control over their destiny, the Arabs then tried to cut off the flow of oil to the West. OPEC would reduce oil production by five per cent a month until America stopped resupplying the Israeli army. The West threw a wobbler, stock markets crashed, all sorts of placatory deals were brokered with the Arabs, and gradually the oil flow resumed. In a sense the oil embargo scared the West too much. America began to take an increasingly active interest in the region. The general feeling was that, come what may, no more fucking around with oil supplies even if it meant recolonising the whole area. Some Israelis started to realise that at some time in the indeterminate future a peace with the Arabs would have to be settled. It was just such a bore fighting these idiots every six years or so. Also it was noted that American support was by no means unconditional and, if it ever came to a choice between oil or Israel, no guarantees were on offer.

Egypt was getting bored of being ignored and President Sadat was actually getting jealous of Saudi's increasingly high-profile role. Something needed to be done, but something big, a real headline grabber. First he kicked out all his Soviet advisors, which really puzzled the Americans since it was a foreign policy coup of the first order for them, and they hadn't actually done anything for Egypt. Then Sadat flew to Jerusalem in 1977 to meet the Israelis. One of the most unexpected things an Arab has ever done. The Arab League promptly kicked Egypt out – this kind of nonsense was not to be tolerated. Egypt made peace with Israel, but it was not a peace the Arab world could tolerate. Sadat got very little, Israel got a good deal and the Palestinian problem was ignored. Egypt had dealt herself out of the Middle East for a worthless piece of paper and a lot of hot air about the future. Sadat was assassinated and no great surprise that was either.

Then at the end of the Seventies America's favourite buddy went completely crackers. 'Progressive friendly Iran', the Americans' big anti-Soviet and 'rapidly modernising' ally, experienced the most peculiar revolution since the late Middle Ages. Beards were *back*, the Shah was exiled, the Islamic republic established and America could do absolutely nothing about it. This was one of the greatest foreign policy setbacks the Americans suffered in the twentieth century. They cast around for a new friend and were pretty pleased when Iraq invaded Iran. Even if they did set it up.

THE 1980s

American strategy was to divide the Middle East, and keep it so structured as to be incapable of co-ordinated action against Israeli or American interests. After Iran had turned itself into the geo-political equivalent of a zoo animal, Saudi Arabia was America's new mainstay in the region. The Saudi government could do practically anything without being criticised by the West, because they were central to the USA's Middle Eastern policy.

The Iran-Iraq war dragged on. The West supplied both sides, ensuring that neither decisively got the upper hand. A drawn-out bloody stalemate kept these two powerful nations on the sidelines for much of the Eighties. Coincidentally enough, this meant neither was capable of causing trouble for any of America's allies – Saudi, the Gulf countries and Israel. Israel in particular just loved the Iran-Iraq war. The Israelis have always been jumpy about these two countries, indeed they went so far as to bomb the Iraqi nuclear reactor at Osirek in 1981.

Divide and Rule: the Rich Get Richer

The Eighties was the decade when the policy of division by envy really began to bite in the Middle East. Whether this was part of a deliberate Western strategy, or a simple by-product of spiralling oil revenues, the effects were the same. The oil-rich countries became increasingly wealthy, increasingly resented by their poorer, more populous neighbours and therefore more dependent on American protection. As oil prices rocketed, the oil states became a byword for rich and lavish living. The spin-off benefits for the West, in the form of increased arms sales, building contracts and infrastructure construction meant the price hikes were no big deal. In fact the revenue generated was actually a stimulus to Western economies throughout the Eighties. This is where the policy of division pays its dues. The rich Arabs imported more and more from the West, as often as not stuff they were incapable of maintaining, so they had to employ foreign 'experts' to keep the infrastructure they had already paid for running.

So the Middle East was fragmenting along economic lines, hardly surprising when the per capita income in Egypt was about 500 dollars and in the UAE it had got as high as 21,000 dollars. This split was made damagingly apparent when the Gulf Co-operation Council was formed in the Eighties, a rich pro-Western alliance of Saudi Arabia and the oil emirates. Arab intellectuals noted sadly that the oil-rich kingdoms were splashing out money on themselves and not doing anything tangible to improve life for the masses in the Middle East without access to oil money.

Elsewhere things were going badly wrong. The oil-rich countries were sucking in skilled labour from all over the Middle East. Egyptian, Jordanian and Palestinian professionals were leaving their own countries in droves. The poor parts of the Middle East were becoming economic clients of the rich, and as such their own economies were distorting. Inflation set in as prices rose to levels that only those with relatives working in the Gulf could afford. Unemployment was rising and unrest was becoming very widespread. In Lebanon a kind of low-level factional civil war which had rumbled on since the mid-Seventies turned much more serious as first Syria then, in 1982, the Israelis invaded. The Israeli agenda was to root out the Palestinians who were involved in the civil war. The stated aim was to move the Palestinians back twenty-five miles from the border, in itself a thoroughly illegal move, but the Israelis went instead for a full-scale invasion, bombing Beirut and colluding in the slaughter of Palestinian refugees in their camps. Lebanon went batshit, America got involved but they forgot to back a faction, which was considered cheating, so they got bombed out. The Lebanese kept at each other. Everyone was getting pretty grumpy.

THE 1990s

The quest to 'lead' the Arab world is a constant. Most countries rule themselves out by being too small and/or preposterous. By the start of the 1990s Egypt was out of the running as no one was speaking to them, Saudi was morally discredited, seen in the region as an American stooge. Someone thought he was going to be a great Arab leader, the new Nasser. And that someone was Saddam Hussein, the Iraqi leader still in power after the debilitating war with Iran, with a nifty line in anti-Israeli rhetoric and a very large army. No one seemed too pleased by this development. Saddam wasn't wildly popular in the Middle East and Iraq was too militarily powerful to please the Saudis.

Paradoxically (or more probably not) what sparked all the trouble was a series of alliances. The Gulf countries had formed the Gulf Co-operation Council, not in itself important except for the reaction it provoked. The ACC (Arab Co-operation Council) was formed in 1989 because Saddam felt snubbed that he wasn't invited to join the GCC, having in his view protected Saudi and Kuwait from Iranian aggression. This new grouping comprised Iraq, Jordan, Egypt (which was thus tacitly re-admitted to the world of Arab politics) and Yemen. Saudi and Kuwait looked on this grouping and found it menacing. They stepped up the arms buying and joint military exercises. Anyway, a lot of griping and sniping between Iraq and Kuwait over unpaid debts and Kuwaiti drilling for oil in moderately disputed areas led to what at first appeared to be a standard burst of rhetoric threatening Kuwait. The Americans misread the situation and sought to calm down Saddam, but accidentally (unless you are an avid conspiracy theorist) gave the impression that they weren't too bothered. Saddam took this as a green light and invaded Kuwait.

The whole Arab world blew a fuse and had a series of messy and inconclusive conferences, trying to get the tangle sorted out before the Americans got involved. The Americans were pressurising Saudi to open their military bases, the Saudis were humming and hawing. All the other Arab countries were shouting their heads off, phoning each other, meeting, threatening, compromising, and then the Saudis cracked. The Americans pointed out that Saddam might be considering invading Saudi itself – no real evidence for this existed but from the past performance of the Saudi army it is pretty certain that the Iraqis wouldn't have had much more difficulty there than in Kuwait. The Americans piled in under the fig leaf of a coalition, the weirdest countries sent token forces and then, as we all saw on television, Iraq was smashed to pieces. Down but not out, Iraq remains a sore on the collective consciousness of the Middle East, another grievance just waiting to cause trouble.

The Peace Process

Something really had to be done about the Palestinians, they had been gloomily littering the Middle East for years. After the Gulf War, the idea was to 'kick them while they're down and weak'. So Arafat was eventually bullied into shaking Itzhak Rabin's hand. They had been stuck in Norway, and the sheer tedium of Norwegian life seems to have got to Arafat. He signed away practically everything, for the sort of right to a sort of entity which might be sort of independent. Unless they were naughty, in which case the Israelis would invade again. This 'entity' was stuffed down the Palestinians' throats: not exactly a state, more a state of mind. Arafat became the elected leader of 'PaleStein': the worst bits of the West Bank, Gaza, no water rights and no removal of Israeli settlers. Jerusalem was effectively ceded. A lousy deal for the Pals but they are probably quite used to getting shafted by now.

The Israelis didn't like the deal either. A fair percentage of Israelis think that Palestinians should simply go away or die. You occasionally hear without a hint of irony Israelis going on about a 'Final Solution' to the Palestinian problem – they of all people should know who that sounds like.

In Other Places

Algeria went berserk in the 1990s and is still having a complicated civil war between the Islamicists and the government that shows no signs of calming down. Unrest is spreading in Egypt. This involves mostly a combination of clampdowns, amnesties, riots and bombs – low-level stuff thus far. Yemen had for so long alternated between wanting to unite North and South and wars between the two that it was a complete surprise, even to the Yemenis, when they actually united in 1990. They had a civil war to celebrate. This one just infuriated all the commentators, who simply couldn't make sense of what this bunch were on about.

All in all the Middle East is in a febrile and resentful mess. The spark that might light the whole fuse is Bahrain. The troubles in a small island state may not seem the most likely catalyst for the next big Middle East blow-up but watch that space.

Politics

Arab political debate seems to be fiendishly complicated and to consist of civil wars, coup d'états, assassinations, riots, argumentative conferences, summits and, of course, lots of shouting. These in general are what you might call the open side of the debating process. In reality most problems are sorted out by negotiation, bribery, hostage taking and horse trading. Just like Europe really. When the political system stops working the riot is the means of modifying the status quo – much as it was in seventeenth- and eighteenth-century England, so don't knock it. Stay away from riots though – you tend to be conspicuous and may well get turned over in the general kerfuffle. Easy enough to spot one brewing up. Knots of people shouting are in general to be avoided. Don't hang around if you see cops in unusual uniforms sitting in lorries. Almost inevitably they are riot control police who will tear-gas the street, each other, the rioters and you, in no particular order of preference, then let off a veritable fusillade of ill-directed small-arms fire. One to avoid.

But Do They Really Love Me?

Depends where you are really. Most Arab leaders have 99.9 per cent recurring majorities and you either have a power-crazed nutter in control or a time-serving corrupt nutter in control. Latter are generally better. As they say of President-For-Eternity Assad, the ballot paper has two options: President Assad or 'Inform next of kin'. Arab leaders seem to become both complacent and paranoid, employing a million informers just to double-check that those 99.9 per cent *really* do care. When all the reports come back: 'Agent Ali Baba found the inhabitants of Dork sacrificing girl children in front of our noble leaders portrait' they begin to believe it. Sadat believed for years that his drunken, three-hour-long, fireside chats on national television were watched and loved by the entire population, who all wandered around quoting his platitudes for days afterwards. That was, he believed it until he got assassinated. Tricky devils, these 0.1 per cent, they seem to get everywhere.

Am I an Imperialist then?

Expect to run into a bit of this chip-on-the-shoulder nonsense, just take it in good part. European involvement has not exactly been welcome to the area and occasionally you have to pick up a bit of the tab. Fair enough.

Political Incorrectness

It is always incorrect to discuss the politics of the country you are in, especially if someone in dark glasses with a little notebook keeps asking your opinion.

What We Want

'What we want is not a united Arabia but a weak and divided Arabia split into little principalities as far as possible under our suzerainty – but incapable of co-ordinated action against us.'

This was explicit British imperial policy in 1919 and is pretty much American-Israeli policy today. Old policies never die, they just change their owners.

Analysis

Whitey has got an arm lock on the Arabs and is planning on keeping it that way.

Arabs have got a chip on their shoulders but are planning to do something about it.

Bit of a classic stalemate.

Coups

These are often brokered from outside the region. It's impossible to believe America isn't fomenting coup plots against Iraq at the moment. The West, or more specifically Britain and the US, has a bad track record for sponsoring coups. The consequences of these actions, however, are never fully thought through. Whoever was responsible for Colonel Gaddafi's coup against King Idris must have ended up feeling like a right idiot. And as for the French meddling in Iran which led to the Ayatollah Khomeini's return . . . There will be a few secret agents looking at unemployment or worse on the strength of that bright idea. The problem is an obvious one – someone who wants to lead a coup d'état is by definition a power-crazed nutter; installing such folk and then hoping they'll 'be your friend' is, well, deluded. Real hello clouds, hello sky school of international diplomacy.

The Textbook

This has been out of print for years, mostly because it worked too well, as a whole generation of Arab leaders would no doubt testify. *Coup D'état* by Edward Luttwak — a 'Teach Yourself' book with attitude.

Assassination

The cutting edge of democracy in the region. Assassination is a legitimate tool of protest in pre-democratic societies. It keeps the top men on their toes, provides employment for armies of policemen, and gives informers some useful ways of getting back at their irritating neighbours. Sort of a check and balance system.

Weird Beards

Beards are a bit more than a simple fashion statement in the Middle East. These days, beards = religion. As a result the response to a bomb attack is, 'Okay, round up the guys with the beards.' Cunning tacticians that the fundamentalists are, they have started shaving. Presumably the whole thing will flip over eventually and you'll have to worry more if you see a clean-shaven Arab than a bearded one. Moustaches however are neutral, nearly everyone has one.

Kidnap

If you are kidnapped, first thing to work out is who has got you and why? No point pretending to be a devout Moslem if you've been captured by a Christian militia. Another one to eliminate from enquiries is that this isn't simply some group of local bores who are reluctant to let a house guest leave until they have unloaded whatever hotch-potch of ill-informed prejudice constitutes their minds. Odds are though, it will be our old friends the Islamic fanatics. Big mistake – if you haven't cancelled those standing orders, you are going to be in serious financial trouble. Big mistake all round. A bore in lousy conditions, sporadic biffings when the captors get in the mood and five years of having the Koran screamed in your ear by a bunch of seriously misguided individuals is going to be pretty unpleasant.

The standard advice on kidnapping sounds so obvious – it is, simply, not to let it start. Your best chance of escape is at the moment of your capture. Things are disorganised and being done at a rush while you are out in public. Once you are in the car with a gun pointed at you, your options begin to decrease pretty radically, and once you are fifty miles away chained to a pipe in a locked basement wearing a blindfold then your chances of escape have passed you by. By this stage in the proceedings you can eliminate the feeble hope that this is simply some form of insistent Arab hospitality. The trouble is that the whole thing happens so quickly. If you reacted with an immediate assault every time someone grabbed you there wouldn't be a walking hotel tout left in the Middle East. If you think you are being snatched, try to make a run for it, interposing as many Arabs between you and your potential captors as is possible. You'll be surprised – however much of a slob you are, you've still got one ten-second 100-metre dash in you. Don't for God's sake try reasoning (reason? With people who would keep Terry Waite in their house for five years?), or a late imperialist, 'straight-right to the dusky jaw' – if there are guns in the equation this equals trouble. Wriggle and then sprint and good luck. It's worth bearing in mind that butting hasn't been invented in the Middle East for some reason and putting the head on someone could give you that vital extra nanosecond as no Arab ever seems to expect it.

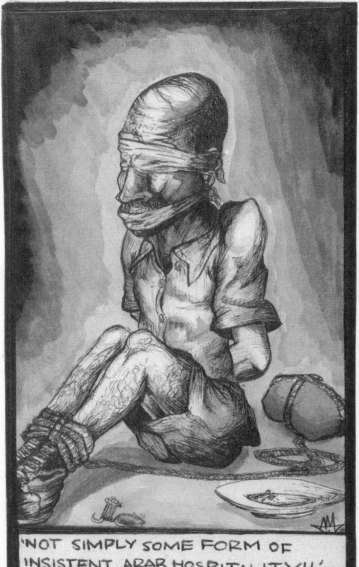

'NOT SIMPLY SOME FORM OF
INSISTENT ARAB HOSPITALITY!!'

These days it is worth thinking about why someone is inviting you to his house. Serious-looking 'students' who don't really seem to approve of you are ones to be particularly suspicious of when they suddenly suggest you visit their family house. Anyone who suggests you might like to drop round for a 'chat' about Islam with some 'friends' in a slum twenty kilometres from where you are staying . . . Well, you'll feel like a total imbecile if you turn up for dinner bringing a cake as a present and find you have paid a taxi to deliver you to your captors for the next five years.

Terrorist Supplement

Those who are targeting tourists, but can't aim: Egypt and Yemen (sometimes: in general they are just targeting anyone).

Those who are targeting foreigners and can aim: Algeria.

Those who aren't targeting foreigners but won't give you a visa: Saudi Arabia, Sudan and Libya.

Those who aren't targeting tourists but are suppressing some virulent minority and might shoot you if you pop up in the middle: Turkey, Iraq and Israel.

Those who have recently stopped targeting tourists, but are re-considering: Lebanon.

Those that require so many foreigners to run their dingbat countries that targeting them would lead to complete economic collapse: Qatar, the Emirates and Kuwait.

Those that are targeting tourists to buy ethnic junk at absurd prices: all of the above.

Getting Bombed

Bombs are exceedingly rare, and if you're not going to a country because of a few bombs you really should just stay at home anyway and buy yourself some nice new window locks. In percentage terms it is a lot less likely than being killed watching a bullfight in Spain and about the same as being hit by a meteorite in the street when you go out to buy your nerd's guide to imaginary fears. So don't even think about it.

Remember you've gone to the Middle East to get Bombed, not bombed.

Economics

The Middle East contains too many people, too much oil, too little water, and imports far too much of what it thinks it needs.

TOO MANY PEOPLE

Most Middle East countries have too many people for the available agricultural land. Arab birth-rates are high with populations rocketing, unemployment runs as high as 30 per cent and the cities are wildly overcrowded. Living standards in the Middle East have been dropping since the mid-1980s. Of course, in such conditions tempers do fray, there is a lot of resentment and disillusionment buried not too far under the surface. Traditionalists that Arab governments are, they resort to systematic repression to keep the lid on it all.

TOO MUCH OIL

And in the wrong places. Oil tends to be in not particularly populous countries. This is great if you are a Kuwaiti as there is plenty of money for all 200,000 of you, but the really teeming poor parts of the Middle East don't produce enough petrol to fill a Ronson, and though there is a certain amount of money donated from the oil-rich states it is nowhere near enough to stop the Gulf Arabs being resented and ridiculed. The combination of wealth and low, unskilled populations makes Gulf Arabs very security-conscious and they are forever buying expensive military kit to protect themselves. Really it is whistling in the dark. The best they can hope for in the face of attack is to hold on for long enough for the Americans to deploy – after seeing the Kuwaiti leader's sprint south the moment the Iraqis invaded, this seems an increasingly forlorn hope.

Oil does coincide with populous countries in a couple of cases – Iraq and Iran being the most obvious. It is difficult to assess what good it has done either country. Again, the overriding priority was to build up huge armies, and to undertake ill-considered capital projects.

TOO LITTLE WATER

The rent-a-cliché on this one is that 'the next war in the Middle East will not be over oil but water'. It could even be true. Smart countries like Turkey and Israel have spent their spare time gaining control of all the water they can while their downstream neighbours were using oil revenues to buy enormous amounts of arms. Turkey has been particularly clever (sneaky or scummy if you are sitting downstream). They have put an extensive dam system, for irrigation of course, on the Tigris and Euphrates. The Iraqis didn't pay enough attention until it was too late and now Turkey in effect can regulate (and perhaps cut off) all Iraq's water whenever it pleases. This has just started to cause considerable irritation downstream where the thought that the only river running through the country might be converted into a dry ditch at short notice is pissing everyone right off.

Other flashpoints could be between Israel and Syria. The Golan Heights is not just strategically important – whoever controls it controls a lot of the meagre supply of water in the region. The Israelis are also tapping the ground water on the West Bank, which means Palestinians will just have to learn to live without. Egypt spent most of the Fifties and Sixties building the enormous Aswan Dam. This was necessary if water supplies were going to keep up with population growth, but it is becoming a bit of a problem. It is the one thing in the Middle East that *must not* fall down. And as it was built by indifferent Russians to sub-Chernobyl standards with Egyptian labour . . . I mean, Egypt could do with a wash and all that but the idea of a tidal wave containing fifty million distressed Egyptians hitting Cyprus, perish the thought.

And now there are new water worries. The most *outré* comes from Libya, which has come up with the idea of tapping desert aquifers (underground fossil water) and piping the results to Tripoli. It is just possible that these desert aquifers are connected to the Nile and if that is the case the Egyptians are going to invade Libya immediately and make Gaddafi into the world's ugliest doner kebab.

Of course the Nile runs through Sudan as well and one thing Sudan could really use is a dam. If, however, they put one brick down the Egyptians will throw a belter, the idea of regulating the Nile flow from outside Egypt being one thing they will go to war on any day of the week.

THE GREAT LEAP FORWARD

The undoubted 'star' of the region is Turkey, which can actually manufacture quite complicated things, at about the level of Britain, to choose another Mickey-Mouse economy. Egypt makes all sorts of things, mostly useless. Yemeni manufacturing is stuck at the Old Testament level and everywhere else is somewhere in between.

The rich Gulf states have managed to prove conclusively that money does not equal economic growth. In fact it often seems that the Gulf Arabs have developed an economic model based on collective insanity. Did you know that in the mid-Eighties Saudi Arabia was the world's sixth biggest exporter of wheat? And that it exported to Switzerland so they could make croissants out of it? Subsidy is the missing word from the equation. It is obviously ruinously expensive to grow wheat in the middle of a desert so the Saudi government decided to subsidise the production of wheat to the extent that it became economic to irrigate sand dunes. In economic terms it is the equivalent of trying to grow cocoa in Shetland. The Gulf economies make no sense whatsoever but operate because you can subsidise everything else from oil revenues. Even so, Saudi Arabia is virtually bankrupt which, considering the amount of oil they have is, well, strange to say the least.

Nasser once said that he wanted to make Egypt the Japan of Africa. This was in the 1950s. As to any economic similarities between Egypt and Japan in the 1990s ... very long pause. None whatsoever. Manufactured Egyptian goods are exported; they have a beer called Stella Export so it must go somewhere. It is revolting, but it may be a number one bestseller in ... Burkina-Faso? ... The Solomon Islands? Somewhere where the locals can't dissolve shoe polish in petrol for themselves anyway.

THE SKILLS GAP

A Saudi was asked if sex was work or fun. He thought for a moment. 'Fun,' he replied. 'If it was work I would get a Philippino to do it for me.' Saudis and Gulfies have got serious attitude problems when it comes to working. They employ third country nationals to do virtually everything and are now running an economy based on south-east Asia and America, which will lead to some bizarre archaeological finds in the future, but never mind. It drives the more sensible rulers of the region bats. The Emir of Kuwait is always banging on about how lazy and decadent the Kuwaitis are, but it is somewhat tricky to talk rich layabouts into taking up shitty jobs. Understandable enough, but if none of your nationals are prepared to clean toilets you are going to be in trouble when the shit hits the fan. The sheer difficulty of getting a Qatari to actually *do* anything defies belief – they might lower themselves to be pilots (fighter only) or newsreaders on the television, but that is the extent of the trickle-down economy.

So why won't the Qataris employ surplus Egyptians? Because they think that they'll apply for residence and, being more sensible, hardworking and intelligent, drive the resident Qataris out. When it comes to a head-to-head job competition the doziest Egyptian on the planet is better qualified than the most educated Qatari. So you've got a 'nation' where no one is even qualified to be a street sweeper but everyone is really rich. So how do you vote when it comes to giving out visas? To much better educated outsiders? Who speak the same language? Have the same religion and, in general, if they were running the country would say, 'Here's a mop. That's a toilet. Get back to me once you've worked out how to clean it.' You employ North Koreans, that's what you do. Economics is an exact science after all. Do the educated poor Arabs resent this? Need you ask? If you do, go and have a look at the Qatari Museum of Heritage. These people have a three-hundred-year history of being dummies. They aren't quite dippy enough to give visas to clever people but they are nice 'n' rich. So you can piss off all you Palestinian PhDs wanting residence permits, or, God forbid, Qatari nationality.

Real Industries

So what do Arabs do all day? The visitor's impression is that Arab men simply sit around in cafés and business consists entirely of selling imported bits of trash to each other. Other than this – a lot work in the public sector as underpaid teachers and officials, their salaries often months, sometimes years, in arrears. A lot work in other countries: Yemen at one stage was running an economy (economy?) where over 90 per cent of the money in the country came from the remittances of people working overseas. A lot of people are unemployed – north Africa especially is cursed with surplus nationals. The final category is those who work the land. Arabs (to their great credit) dislike working intensely. As soon as any Arab is solvent he retires. Manual labour is done only by the abjectly poor. A working Arab likes to sit behind a desk and do fuck-all, all day and every day. If he gets a uniform and a telephone or two he is just about in heaven.

Heavy industry does exist: Saudi has some of the biggest petrochemical plants in the world but they couldn't be run without foreigners – poor ones to do the dirty bits and Europeans and Americans to do the complex bits. Lots of Saudis are employed but, as I said, they sit behind desks and do fuck-all, all day and every day. There are some bizarre-looking factories in Egypt making God knows what standard of concrete and iron.

Surreal Industries

Tourism is the one for this – in many Arab countries *you* are route number one out of the bread queue.

Err on the side of caution if someone approaches you speaking English. He may be simply wanting to practise his English but the odds are he wants you to come and buy something. Not necessarily a bad thing to happen, you may indeed fancy whiling away a couple of hours bargaining for something you don't much want. Just bear in mind someone's motivation for talking to you in fluent English may not be altruism (seems a bit obvious). It may be that you are seen as a form of 'Opportunity Knocks' (or from your point of view should that be 'Importunity Sucks?').

BREAD

To live people need to eat. Subsidy is the (incorrect) answer from Morocco all the way round to Syria and Iraq. Governments are haemorrhaging money subsidising the price of bread and other essentials, but they can't stop.

In Algeria when they hiked the bread price in the Eighties, the subsequent rioting left hundreds dead and, not that indirectly, led to the upsurge in support for the Islamic Salvation Front and the current civil war. Egypt cannot afford to raise subsidised prices. Every time it has done so rioting has broken out and the raises have had to be reversed. The governments can't afford the subsidies, so they have to borrow, and the population keeps growing, and the yield from the small percentage of arable land available can't keep up. So they have to buy imported wheat at world prices (impossibly expensive) or buy from the Americans on the quasi-imperialist USAID programmes, so they become more dependent on America, so the people hate them more as governments are forced to adopt more pro-American policies.

Bit of a bummer really this post-imperialism.

And Circuses

Or how forty hours a week of women's volleyball or tennis, plus a few slow and vaguely sexy American soaps keep the troops subdued. American pro-wrestling is very popular too. I assume the Roman gladiators fixed bouts in advance as well.

Arab television is bizarre and, because the programming is relatively naive, you can spot its attempts to keep the downtrodden trodden down.

Soil Bank

How to grow enough to feed an expanding population from a diminishing base of agricultural land. Desertification has been going on for a long time; one look at all those abandoned Roman cities in north Africa is enough to tell you that when they were built they weren't in the middle of the desert. In Roman times Egypt and north Africa were the providers of grain for the empire. Rome only became untenable when it lost these provinces in the fourth century.

Nowadays the situation is reversed. Some 60 per cent of Libya's food is imported, Saudi is at 70 per cent and Egypt is between 40 and 45 per cent. Even these figures, alarming enough as they are, do not give the full picture. The big cities are even more heavily dependent on imports, partly because they don't have any agricultural sector worth mentioning but mostly because the expectations of city dwellers are much higher than those of rural communities. The main food supplier to the region is America (oh-oh).

Fundamentally Flawed

Downtown Cairo, air looks like diluted vomit this morning. Pollution ain't in it, it's like a 3-D Jackson Pollock. This town is a mess, sixteen million dusky losers slogging it out in the Mother of all Buttholes. The town is so shoddily constructed that a good belch can knock down a tower block. Yet crime is virtually unheard of and the poorest raggedy man will drag you into his house and give you as high a percentage of his possessions as he can force you to accept. What can you do? You want to give him something but it's obviously a bit naff just to peel off a couple of notes at the end of dinner. Think ahead, carry small gifts, anything pleases and something for the children goes down particularly well.

Looks like a good time for that 'See Egypt and die' holiday of a lifetime. Cairo is now famous not just for pyramids and squalor, but now it has the bearded wonders. Book early, prices are down to the bone. Not that bad really. Cairo has been experiencing a wave of bomb attacks, but what a wave. The government claims these fiends are being trained in Iran and Afghanistan. They should ask for their money back. How anyone, however ill-trained, can blow his own foot off in a mortar attack escapes me. Maybe Egyptians are just too nice to be really ruthless — blowing themselves up in public seems to be as nasty as they can manage. Times have to be hellish hard before Egyptians get so agitated. Normally the kindest and most welcoming people, these days there's an exciting background tension. You are continually thinking, 'Will this push things over the edge?' One feels something will, but what does it take? And when will it happen? Will I get lynched on my way home from the pub? Or will a man I've never met before suddenly give me flowers, feel me up and tell me I look like Robert Redford? Thanks, but no thanks, eh.

It's too much fun even to bother going to the Pyramids, which show a distinct lack of imagination. (Surely with all that labour they might have come up with something slightly more creative?) Just hang around in town drinking muddy coffee and listen to the rumour mill going into overdrive. Cairenes take their gossip seriously, the only prerequisite is wild inaccuracy. After a recent earthquake, rumour had it that the Israelis had nuked Cairo and the government was covering it up. (Why? I ask myself.) Newspapers are pretty drab fare by comparison.

You are in far greater danger from the ubiquitous vendors of pseudo-Pharaonic crap, who'll make your life a misery from the word go. As a tourist be warned that being addressed as 'my friend' has the same validity as being called 'Pal' in a Scottish pub when folk are breaking their glasses into jagged weapons. To the credit of Egyptians the subsequent damage will in general be purely financial. You might as well resign yourself to being systematically overcharged. This is not quite as straightforward as it appears. In general you pay according to your assumed status. Rich Egyptians probably pay more or less what you do, poor ones much less. So it is not always necessary to scream blue murder just because the guy at the next table has paid half what you did to have his shoes cleaned. Though God knows far too many tourists do.

Different rules apply at major tourist sights. Just hit anyone who comes within range.

Single European ladies, unless spectacularly deformed, should avoid even touching cigarette packets in public. It leads to near immolation as a scrum four-deep flashing fake Ronsons, will have the eyebrows off you (for starters).

Try the archaeological museum – don't be put off by the petrol bombers who 'have a go' every other day. Some humorist has rewritten the book for Molotov Cocktails – it now reads: 'Light blue touch paper and expire.' So it's not a big problem unless you have aesthetic objections to semi-incinerated Egyptians littering the streets. The Ancient Egyptians should carry a sanity warning: pure science fiction. What were they playing at?

'Oh look, another Jackal-headed statue. A monumental inscribed foot; splendid.'

No one ever seems to have worked out what they were going on about. Pig out in the museum on peculiar artifacts until you feel your eyes start to glaze over.

Back out in the public sector. How do Egyptians stand it? They remain remorselessly good-humoured while all around them things fall apart. Two societies? In Egypt money has practically created two distinct species – the fat cats and tourists consuming away like crazy while the losers are living on 20 pence a month eating time-expired offal in a cardboard box. The two exist side by side, just to rub the have-nots' noses in it. They sit in bizarre poverty watching crooks in their bribe-bought Mercedes flitting in and out of pseudo-European hot-spots, or some overweight tourist spending the equivalent of a month's wages on a meal. Surprised that they don't riot every day.

Things are starting to boil though . . .

On a Need-to-know Basis

INSHALLAH

One of the first and almost certainly the most meaningless words you will learn in Arabic. In strictly religious terms it means something along the lines of 'If God wills it', but in practical terms it can mean anything from 'I haven't got a clue' to 'Who cares' or 'I can't be bothered turning up tomorrow'. Basically a warning signal – if an Arab says, 'I'll see you tomorrow, inshallah', unless he is a religious type he isn't turning up.

BUILDING BLOCKS

The Middle East is full of modern buildings built of shoddy materials. Tower blocks are sometimes built without proper foundations. Theory seems to have been that they still looked like buildings. I mean if you photographed them they looked exactly like the tower blocks in Murmansk so they should be alright. This, combined with concrete which was little more than sand dyed grey, makes for some ridiculous collapses. Blocks of flats which dissolve into clouds of dust if a kid pisses against the side of them, that kind of thing. An exaggeration, of course, but in the case of something unexpected such as a gas explosion, buildings tend to collapse all over the place.

To be fair this is not simply an Arab problem, some of the tower blocks put up in Britain have proved remarkably vulnerable to minor explosions which in a properly constructed block would not have levelled the bloody thing. But dodgy building standards are the rule rather than the exception throughout the Middle East. This, coupled with a disregard for building regulations which is outright criminal in many cities, means that high-rises get planning permission for eight storeys and by the time they eventually collapse have ended up being eleven storeys high. Onwards and upwards is just so tempting – the top of a tower block is flat and much the same size as the bottom of it, so why buy more land? A couple more floors won't hurt . . .

CUT AND DRIED

Censorship is not always a joke in the Middle East – this particularly applies to cartoonists. Mocking the leaders or powerful figures can have serious consequences. In societies where literacy rates are low, cartoons can have an effect disproportionate to their actual content. Also vulnerable are Arab intellectuals who speak their minds. Edward Said's comments on the Palestinian state and Arafat's methods of government could have made it unsafe for him to return to the occupied territories. So even a big international reputation is no sure protection against the wrath of undemocratic leaders and Palestine is hardly the most repressive regime in the Middle East.

Elsewhere things are worse. Abdulatif Laabi was sentenced to ten years of imprisonment and torture in Morocco for 'Crimes of Opinion'. Whatever the opinions were, they presumably didn't justify ten years. Even after his release he was forced into exile. He is just one eminent example of how censorship and the fear of speaking your mind permeates the Middle East like a virus. Protest in any form or an honest statement of opinion can be risky, and risky can mean fatal. This is part of the reason there are so many Arab exiles. Even living overseas, these exiles are running a bit scared. Some regimes don't like dissidents getting away with anything. Libya, Iran and Iraq in particular have been responsible for harassing and even killing exiles in Europe. What happens to dissidents inside these countries doesn't bear thinking about. It is a brave man or woman who puts his neck on the block by complaining, or poking fun at the government.

In some countries even talking to foreigners can arouse the suspicion of the authorities. This applies in Libya, Iraq, the occupied territories and probably in Iran and Saudi too. A certain degree of paranoia and an ability to unconsciously practise double-think is an important aspect of survival skills for any Arab. If you are standing at some military base dressed in ill-fitting uniforms on 50 pence a month listening to the collected speeches of our noble leader for hours on the trot, being able to demonstrate an enthusiasm you don't really feel is probably essential for your future well-being. You may grouse privately, but if it comes to the end of the speech and you actually say, 'What a load of cobblers', your military career is going to have an immediate unhappy ending. Even in private it may be dangerous to express opinion – many regimes depend very heavily on the use of informers and there is pressure put on these informers to come up with names.

It's a bind for Arabs. Who can they trust outside their immediate family? Some become so frustrated that they confide in foreigners, reasoning that they can be pretty sure they are not employed by internal security. That is partly why talking to foreigners can arouse suspicion. In some ways it is like the old Soviet Union

– a lot of Arab security forces were trained by east Europeans and Arab leaders prefer to keep a very tight rein on expressions of opinion. There is a craving for actual news – Arabs hear rumours all the time. Rumours that don't in the least correspond with what is published in the newspapers. So gossip becomes a sort of inaccurate and dangerous lifeline. On the other hand many just play it safe and *never* mention the leader of the country or politics in any shape or form.

A word Arabs dread is 'police'. Try it if someone is hassling you anywhere from Rabat to Oman, say the magic word and nine times out of ten you won't see them for dust.

If you get ten years for crimes of opinion, hacking off sources of foreign currency might get you God knows how long. It's pretty dismal stuff really. This again takes us back to the influx of Arab refugees to Europe – they are tenacious once they are here because being sent back with an 'illegal immigrant' tag is like tattooing 'torture me' on their foreheads. Algerians are particularly averse to going home, for obvious reasons. Same applies to Iraqis, you need to be pretty desperate to go hijacking planes rather than go home to sunny Iraq. There is an odd side-effect here – even in the most whacked out police states, the one place it is definitely safe to criticise in the Middle East is Israel. So some of the criticism you hear is effectively displacement activity – it doesn't represent a genuine belief that the Israelis are smuggling aphrodisiac bubble gum into Egypt to ruin Egyptian girls. On the surface level you may be listening to an anti-Israeli or anti-American rant but really it is a way of indirectly letting off steam about their own government. Double-think, it's the only way to live, or to live safely, at any rate.

This of course means there is a great deal of tension at the core of Arab societies. Analysing the actual effects of lack of freedom is a dubious business, but in the Arab world it seems to have a cumulative effect, in so far as when an opportunity to really cut loose occurs, they throw an absolute belter. This could be seen at the time of the fall of the hated Shah in Iran. The reaction of the Islamic revolution looked hysterical and even rather terrifying to the West, but ten years living in a police state where you are scared to speak your mind to close friends had built up a level of frustration which couldn't be quantified until it got a chance to blow.

JOYS OF REPRESSION

Government reactions to open dissent are, shall we say, 'firm'. A couple of examples will suffice. In Hama in Syria an armed insurrection of the Moslem Brotherhood in 1982 led to an all-out army assault on the town which may have killed as many as 25,000 and it never made the local papers. At a lower, more day-to-day level: in Cairo the response to a bomb attack is inevitably 'firm'. Suburbs are sealed off, a couple of thousand arrests are made. Those arrested get a good whacking around or a long jail sentence and the television news headline is: 'Egyptian footballer insulted in Zimbabwe'. Any form of protest provokes army intervention. Recently Jordanian bread price hikes provoked riots which one might imagine were handled with our old friend 'firmness'. Certainly previous bread riots while I was in the country accounted for ten dead officially (Jordan has a relatively open media) and 200 in the gossip factory, and who knows which figure was nearer the truth?

ATV

Surreal and upwards and outwards. Arabs seem to watch about nine hours of television a day, and my, is it ever peculiar rubbish. Local stuff can be gripping. Televised hand-chopping was gruesome enough in Yemen but the fact that they seemed to be using one of Bruce Forsyth's old sets made it bizarre in the extreme. Judicial amputation as game show? Well it's an interesting concept. They stopped it after a couple of months, too many people were laughing.

Some countries televise the *hajj* (pilgrimage to Mecca), which makes for good viewing – 100,000 people in white robes circling a black stone for nine hours at a stretch, hmm.

Another feature of Middle Eastern TV is seemingly random cutting, from long, still shots of bulrushes, to alphabet lessons, back to flamingos looking miserable in a pond, to a news broadcast, to adverts, to a bit of a game show to . . . It is the form-without-function problem, giving the impression of channel surfing through the sixty worst channels you've never seen without the least need to reach for the remote control.

Soap Operas

Soaps from America which have been scrapped and the perpetrators rounded up and shot, achieve a sort of hideous twilight existence in the Middle East. *The Bold and the Beautiful* has been running for about three light years in Egypt. In terms of plot and dialogue this would not convince an amoeba, even an Egyptian one, but it does have a fair old number of bulky blondes in short skirts which makes it a sure-fire hit.

Egyptians themselves do a mean soap opera, consisting entirely of interlocked flashbacks and significant phone calls. They go something like this: 'Abdullah . . . (pause),' woman speaking urgently into telephone. Cut to a group of previously unseen

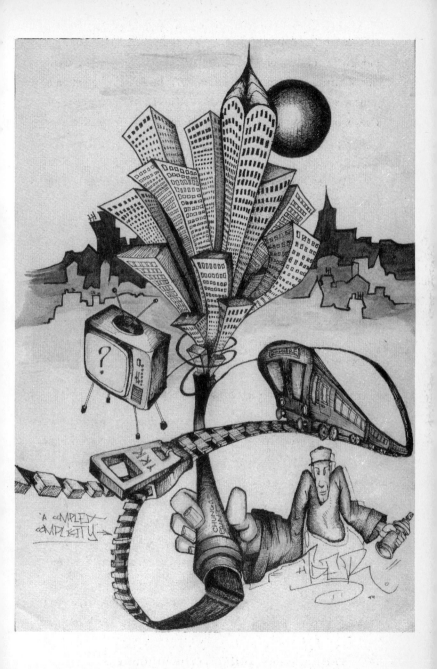

characters having a picnic. The mobile phone rings. Character picks it up 'Abiir . . . (Pause).' By this time you are tearing your hair out; it has clearly been a flashforward as the last phone dated from the 1950s. By now the mind is starting to boggle and then you get another flashback. A man in a white suit is being strangled by someone wearing scuba-diving gear on a beach. Cut to blood-stained rug, with music swelling in the background to some kind of conclusion, cut back to the picnic. Mobile phone rings, he speaks, 'Abiir . . . ?' End of episode. And you are left sitting there, thinking – what the hell are these guys on? I have no idea how anyone can follow what is going on in these things, linear they ain't.

NEWSPAPERS

Imported ones

These are expensive – because the *Financial Times* prints in Germany it is nearly always the cheapest foreign paper available. Excellent paper too, with the added bonus that if you are sitting reading the *FT* no dumb-ass stoner will ever come and bore you about how he made a bong out of his girlfriend's skull after she died during their desert trek.

Local papers in English

Al Ahram weekly in Egypt and *The Jordan Times* in Jordan are good. Others are less so, the *Egyptian Gazette* is daily and contains such quotes as: 'Russian exports of unclear [sic] technology are increasing to the Middle East.' Presumably of the, 'What does this red button do Mohammed?' type. The last words of a whole generation of Arab pilots.

HOT GOSSIP

Newspapers and television are government-controlled and full of astonishingly easily disproved lies, so the whole of the Middle East functions on gossip and rumour. If rumour is to be believed the Middle East is full of Zionist and imperialist agents doing the most bizarre and incredible things. An outbreak of fainting among Jordanian schoolgirls? It was the Zionists, or so they reckoned in the cafés. How had they done it? You've no idea, everything from Zongo Rays beamed from Tel Aviv to secret tunnels under the Dead Sea was considered. Conspiracy theories are everywhere, and no accident can happen without some sage intervening. When a tunnel collapsed in Saudi killing hundreds of pilgrims, the Turks took their turn in the spotlight. They had deliberately built the tunnel to collapse; proof of this was easy – there were tunnels in Turkey, some of which *hadn't* collapsed.

In truth television news is pretty poor – 'Our Noble Leader's Home Videos' is nearer the mark. This is bad enough in important countries but when the major Qatari news headline is: 'Deputy Minister of Sudani Agriculture visits Qatar', complete with shaky camera shots of the visiting minister's knees, it's time to give up. Egyptian news has a more professional air about it.

Censorship

An additional level of censorship has been placed on Arab news by the Saudis, who have bought heavily into Arab media. This has particularly harmed the film industry. It has quite an odd effect in so far as 1950s films are just full of gorgeous-looking Egyptian girls jiggling and pouting most enticingly, whereas modern films are dominated by badly dressed old trouts. The impression is that Egyptian women have got much uglier all of a sudden. Lebanese output is still relatively free of the dead hand of Wahabism, but it is easy to tell that when the babes leave the screens, the Saudis have bought the studio (and probably the babes).

It is actually rather nastier than that. To replace the indigenous product, B American soaps are bought in, so bulky US blondes replace dark-haired temptresses as the Arab man's ideal. Big mistake, but that's the power of television for you.

By the by the Arabic for 'blonde' is, I kid you not, 'shagger'. From where, no doubt, much of the confusion arises.

POOR AND NEEDY/POOR AND GREEDY

Comes to much the same thing. Poor is poor. Some Moroccans would consider being paid a quid to jump up and down on the spot for a couple of hours to be a genuine financial windfall. The trouble is, what some tourists want from Arabs is not as innocuous as that. To get that wonderful thing called money, Arabs end up doing things they don't want to do. This can be anything from sleeping with middle-aged matrons to giving blow jobs to time-expired queens. Or, on a more pragmatic level, serving drink to fat and ill-mannered tourists who, as they get drunker, get ruder. All that smiling and the 'Thank you, sirs' takes a toll on the nerves eventually.

The tourist industry brings some pretty squalid variables into life in the Middle East. Variables with one common factor: we have money by their standards and, in order to induce us to part with it, people will put up with all manner of gross or petty behaviour. Some visitors behave shamefully. Watching ageing

French homosexuals cruising Tunisian secondary schools was frankly disgusting. This sort of thing has an effect on the locals who work in the tourist industry as they themselves begin to sink towards these levels. Many become, by local standards, morally unacceptable. They become outcasts from their own society in the quest for pennies from the rich man's table. So when someone is hassling you, try to keep a civil tongue in your head. The guy may indeed be a fucked-up scumbag, but it was probably association with foreigners which brought him so low in the first place. This having been said, these guys can be irritating, *very* irritating. Their efforts to capture you are remorseless. The gambits change every year: one of the favourites being, 'You will not speak to me . . . [melodramatic pause, eyes hypocritically downcast] because you are a racist!' Fantastic – no middle-class tourist could wriggle out of that one, or steel himself to either reply, 'I am now', or burst into contemptuous laughter, the only known ways of getting rid of the man. I liked invocation of paranoia. The implication is that your refusal to do something dangerous, illegal or clearly stupid was a fault on your part. 'You will not take LSD with me and drive into the desert to buy guns from my Algerian friends at the border . . . I am sorry . . . you are a very paranoid man.'

Yeah, like paranoia rather than commonsense.

BUS RULES

The man who smells most strongly of livestock will always sit beside you.

You will be given handfuls of sweets/tangerines/nuts/melon seeds from practically everybody on the bus.

If you look out of the side windows you'll see scenery. If you look out the front windows you will see imminent death.

Journey times don't matter – a two-hour journey can feel like eternity while a twenty-four-hour one can slip by in a sort of trance.

There is never enough legroom.

There is always some creature of the fields secreted somewhere on the bus.

You will be introduced to it at some stage in the proceedings.

TIME AND INSHALLAH

Planes leave on time. Trains leave at a time written nowhere and one which doesn't in the least resemble any time you might have been told. Buses leave whenever they get in the mood, shared taxis leave two people after you think: this car is too fucking full. Any other comment on time-keeping is superfluous. Except for phrases like 'the train will leave, inshallah'. These mean nothing whatsoever and are certainly not cues for making a rush for the platform from which some humorous liar has told you the train will leave. Trains are the slowest and safest, but tend to stop for hours in the middle of nowhere. One 'don't bother saving fifty pence' type tip – don't go the lowest class on any train in the Middle East unless you are a garrulous masochist. Buses are faster but a bit badly driven. Well quite a bit. Shared inter-city taxis are much faster than they should be and bring meaning to the phrase 'driven to distraction'. Yemen is the worst for gut-wrenching 'Nearer my God to thee' journeys, but there are plenty contenders.

RENT A CAR?

Not always recommended: unless you do most of your driving in Europe at demolition derbies you won't be in with much of a chance. If you do rent a car the following points should be noticed. Traffic lights and road signs are decorations. It is legal to drive anywhere on (or near) the road, at any speed and in any direction. Overtaking is done on blind bends and on one-track roads. If you are facing oncoming traffic on a one-lane road with a cliff on one side and a calamitous drop on the other, the standard protocol is for both drivers to accelerate towards each other, thinking all the time: 'I am a person of the utmost consequence.' The flinch which allows you to pass each other in a shower of wing mirror glass is done in the last five metres. That is, after you've resigned yourself to a hideous death at a combined velocity of near 300 kph. If, as it happens, you've judged the width wrongly, you will both die in one of the crashes which litter the Middle East and look more like bomb outrages. Much like jousting really. If you by any chance survive a crash and your car is operational, leave the scene as quickly as you can. It is considered unsporting not to die in car crashes, survivors are often lynched, especially if you've wiped out any local children or chickens in 'your' crash.

THINGS TO TAKE

Clothes

Loose and cotton should be the basic rules. The heat makes tight clothes uncomfortable. Shirts with collars provide protection for the back of the neck, which is particularly vulnerable to sunburn. A hat is useful for keeping the sun off. For men a couple of pairs of baggy trousers are worth taking as you are often expected to sit on floor cushions and there is no comfortable or modest way of doing this in tight jeans. Women and men should consider dressing more modestly than they do at home. Shorts are seen as pretty scummy outside resort areas; much the same applies to tiny armpit-revealing tops. Women wearing little skirts or tops will get a lot of sexual hassle and in out-of-the-way places will be treated with downright hostility. Immodestly dressed women can get themselves stoned or assaulted by either angry or lust-crazed guys. It's difficult clothes-wise for women, I mean you can't walk around in a shroud. If you are a Western woman you will get hassled even if you dress modestly, but longer skirts than normal are no bad idea – if nothing else, it puts you in a stronger position if you have to complain about someone pestering you. Claiming someone is behaving shamefully towards you is a bit difficult to sustain while you are wearing less clothes than Arab women wear during sex. Balance it out for yourself.

Medical Kit

Most basic things, like sticking plasters and pills, are widely available. Things to consider taking are high-factor sun-block cream (15+) and condoms, as AIDS is quite widespread, especially among the sort of beach-boy Arabs who hang around chasing foreign women and men. If you are on regular medication, take enough to cover your trip with some extra. It is worth carrying your prescription to explain that your drugs are medically necessary and to inform any doctor of what you take regularly in case you fall ill with something else. Glasses are to be preferred to contact lenses as the area is very dusty and this can make contacts irritating to wear long-term.

THINGS NOT TO TAKE

A Walkman for one thing. Israelis seem addicted to taking them to pieces at the border, but they aren't so good at putting them back together again.

If you are going to Israel, don't take any addresses of Palestinian acquaintances into the country.

Don't take booze into the Gulf States, Libya or Saudi.

Pornography will be confiscated, read in secret by the customs officers, I imagine.

Anything lettered in Hebrew or bearing the star of David. Remember this when entering and leaving Israel.

Also, avoid having Palestinian headgear or pro-Palestinian literature at Israeli customs – the least that will happen is that it will be confiscated, and the last thing you want is to be interrogated by Israeli security. If they deem you a suspicious character, they may keep an eye on you for the duration of your stay.

Really flash kit, lap-top computers, camcorders and the like are not entirely sensible. Arabs are generally honest, but why offer temptation to the few local crooks?

THINGS NOT TO TAKE HOME

Antiques are illegal to export and the penalties can be stiff.

Drugs.

Sexually-transmitted diseases and parasites – the kind of souvenir your partner might resent being given.

CARRY INS

Apart from the obvious things to take – clothes, money and passport – there are some out-of-the-way ideas which may not occur to you.

A few photos of your family. These are genuinely of interest to Arabs, and put you in a more human light as far as they are concerned.

A couple of postcards of your home town, which you can give to café owners or whoever – they will display them for ages and think the better of you and your country.

A tie – easily justifies the space. A couple of reasons, one obvious, one less so. Obvious one is dealing with officials; less obvious is if you are invited to an Arab's house it is only polite to at least attempt to look as if you've dressed up for the occasion and short of carrying a three-piece suit a tie is a portable way of smartening yourself up.

A sheet sleeping bag, as lack of sheets/grey sheets are pretty much the rule rather than the exception in cheap hotels.

Women travellers might consider taking a ring to wear on your wedding finger, even if you are not married – it conveys a certain amount of protection from Arab hasslers. Photos of kids in your wallet can re-emphasise your 'married' status. If you don't have any kids, borrow a snap from a friend – babies all look the same anyway. This is a good idea for men as well – if you are over twenty-five and unmarried it will generally be thought that you are gay and you may get sick of being offered small boys at bargain prices.

Certificates, or copies, or forgeries, if you are thinking of picking up some work as you travel.

Take suede shoes, not leather. There is no known way for a street shoe-cleaner to polish suede.

Dog Dazer

This is a relatively new invention – it emits a supersonic howl inaudible to humans but quite adequate to see off all but the most persistent pack of dogs. This is a bit of a godsend in the Middle East, where dogs are an outright nuisance. Whether it would actually see off a rabid dog is another matter, but it might be worth trying. Any comments from survivors would be welcome.

It is not available over the counter in Britain but mail-order costs £34.95 from Dazer UK, 43 Northcote Road, London SW11 1YY (0171) 228 2360.

The sole disadvantage is that the dazer provokes suspicion in customs officers as it appears to be simply an electronic switch – it tends to get confiscated or at least dismantled.

Food

If you are visiting expatriate friends, there is bound to be some form of British food they are missing desperately, it can be anything from herbal tea to Marmite. Ask in advance – you can make yourself a very welcome guest if you bring a bottle of brown sauce for some poor deprived soul in Oman.

Bacon

It's probably worth taking a couple of vacuum packs of bacon –

these may be confiscated at customs, but in most places you won't be troubled over this. Not worth the risk if visiting Saudi or Gulf countries though. These will serve as a hard currency to give to any expatriate you bump into. They will be pathetically grateful and (if you're lucky) put you up for weeks on the strength of your generous gift.

Booze

In countries where you are allowed to take in a couple of bottles for personal consumption, take in brand-label whiskies, even if you don't drink the stuff. Its resale value will probably pay for a two-week binge on local beer. The countries where you can take in at least a litre of alcohol are: Turkey, Egypt, Jordan, Lebanon, Morocco, Tunisia and Bahrain. Customs rules do change at short notice – the most likely to drop off this list in the future is Bahrain and possibly Jordan, so double-check. Even in these countries alcohol sometimes gets confiscated by greedy and/or alcoholic customs officials. All other countries prohibit the import of alcohol. Don't even think about it when arriving in Saudi, Qatar or Libya. You might get away with a bottle entering Syria or Yemen – even if it is discovered you can plead innocence, let it be confiscated and probably suffer no consequences. (That is *probably*, so maybe not too bright an idea if you are starting a two-year contract. Your employer will understandably be furious if you get yourself deported before you even get out of the airport.)

Baggage

If you are roaming around the Middle East, unless you are actually planning on doing a lot of hiking or wadi-walking, a rucksack has a few serious drawbacks. Worst is they are often relegated to roof racks on buses where they are liable to be badly secured and fall off. One soft bag about half full (you'll buy things in transit to fill it up) is about the best. A kitbag isn't bad, with a sort of double-briefcase-size soft bag as hand luggage is a combination worth considering. Anything more is restrictive, so if you are planning to be moving around a lot, try and avoid taking too much luggage.

Caution, My Brothers, Take Heed

Balance security and politeness in this instance. If you want to wear a money belt do so, but inside your clothes. You should also carry a standard wallet which contains your working cash for that day. You are sending out a rather untrusting message if you dig into a concealed money belt to pay for your drinks when among Arab friends.

Hotel Security

Some people like to take a padlock or even wedges to make sure their hotel room can't be broken into. I think this may be going a bit far, you could end up nailing doors shut or fitting window locks to every hotel bedroom in the Middle East. Hotel rooms in the Middle East aren't, as it happens, particularly secure, so you are probably not wise to leave your passport or wads of cash in the room. Passports can be left at reception – in many places they insist on it. Theft is most likely if you are sharing dormitory-style accommodation. Israel is particularly bad for this, but if you are sharing with other budget travellers anywhere, be aware that one common economy measure is to steal from incautious room-mates.

Insurance

Not worth taking out really, it seems like asking for trouble and the traditional scam of insuring your baggage then putting in a claim when you get back doesn't work as often as it used to. Medical insurance might come in handy for the nervous, but only a policy which includes a Medivac option since, if you are really ill, a flight out of the region is the best choice. It's a different story for people living and working in the Middle East – find out from fellow expats who does a good deal.

NON-SMOKERS

The Middle East is a smoking zone – everyone seems to be on about forty a day. People smoke on buses, at petrol stations, in cafés and on trains. This makes the region absolute purgatory for fanatical anti-smokers and, even if you do smoke, sometimes it gets a bit much. In terms of travelling for non-smokers, stick to buses and sit right up at the back as the back door on a bus is nearly always open and you get some ventilation that way. If you open a window it will often be closed again – Arabs aren't too fond of draughts. For non-smokers, shared taxis are virtually impossible. Trains sometimes have non-smoking first-class sections, but everyone ignores the no smoking signs and puffs away. However, first-class rail coaches are air-conditioned, which helps. Arabs are always offering cigarettes, so don't get all ratty even if you are a real anti-smoking nut – the guy is being polite.

The Arabic for 'I don't smoke' is ana la ada*kh*in (emphasis on *kh* as if you were clearing your throat).

The Arabic for 'Will you stop blowing smoke in my face, you

evil polluting devil' does not exist. It is pointless to ask an Arab to stop smoking because it bugs you; he may listen politely but nine times out of ten at the end of the exchange he will still offer you a cigarette. For non-smokers but non-diehards, it is actually worth *carrying* a packet of cigarettes to offer to others, particularly soldiers at check-points who are always after cigarettes. If you crash them a couple of fags, it cheers them up sufficiently to speed you through the check-point.

SMOKERS

This is your kind of area, everyone smokes. It is worth picking up a carton of Marlboro at duty free, even if you despise them as cigarettes or are planning on switching to local brands on arrival. Arabs think they are a real premium smoke and are happy to accept them as gifts.

Most widely available in the Middle East and reliable in terms of cost and freshness are Rothmans, which are locally manufactured. They not only taste different from British Rothmans but vary throughout the region. The tastiest are in Yemen, the least enjoyable are those imported from India. International brands are expensive, but local brands tend to be a bit on the lousy side, though quite smokable. They don't use Virginia tobacco but the sweeter oriental tobacco. The best Egyptian or Turkish tobacco is very high quality, but it is exported and what ends up in the local brands is often of inferior quality.

Turkey has the best quality local cigarettes – the very best and the cheapest are Bitlis non-filter, available only in east Turkey. Quite acceptable filter cigarettes include Bafra Samsun and the higher quality Tekel 2000 brand.

Egypt has Cleopatra, a poor quality mass production cigarette. Smokable, but no better.

Morocco: again the cheapest brands seemed about the best – Casa Sport were not too bad.

Otherwise local brands are a bit of a lottery. Always worth trying a packet, but maybe not finishing it.

WATER PIPES

Variously called *sheesha*, *nargileh* or *meda'a*, these are common in cafés and in private houses. Basically tobacco is placed on hot charcoal, and the smoke is inhaled through a long pipe after the smoke has been cooled by being passed through water. In cafés you pay per smoke. Mouthpieces are a bit unhygienic but if you overcome your scruples (or buy your own mouthpiece) these make for an interesting smoke. A real nicotine-rich hit, the smoke pleasantly cool, the only irritation being Arabs are always chipping in telling you how to use it or just staring at the odd spectacle of a European using a water pipe. They are pretty strong medicine though, not for Silk Cut smokers.

Getting Around

IN TOWN

Shared taxis are common. These follow fixed routes round town stopping where asked. The best are the *dolmuşes* in Istanbul, especially for car freaks. These days the ubiqutous minibuses and Peugeot 505s are beginning to replace the amazing range of 1950s American cars which served as shared taxis. If you like old cars go down to Kadiköy on the Asian side and take the *dolmuş* up to Uskader. Some of the cars on this run are from the Twenties and have running boards. There are some great origin-of-the-species Dodges and Cadillacs patched together by ingenious Turks. Some people consider buying these museum pieces but it is not always recommended as they are virtually rebuilt from scrap and, I was told, are unmaintainable by European mechanics who look at the bizarre reconstituted engines and have to go and lie down with a damp towel over their foreheads.

Driven to Destruction

Arabs are probably the world's worst drivers and those who are compelled to do such demeaning jobs as drive buses have a chip on their shoulder to go with the combination of insane optimism and fatalistic introspection which dogs all Arab drivers. The worst driver in the Middle East who my lady friend of the time quite rightly had jailed − for, hopefully, eternity − is Achmed al

Hajj, who operated out of the main taxi rank in Sana'a on the Sana'a–Taizz run. If this creature is still operating his wretched trade do not under any circumstances enter his car. This is a driver who while overtaking on a blind bend at 100 kph takes it into his head to release the wheel and climb into the back seat to discuss God only knows what with the passengers. How he thought cars stayed on roads escapes me. Put it this way, even the other Yemenis and Sudanese in this taxi were screaming by this stage and God knows they've seen plenty of bad drivers. This man was a rare exception – such people normally die in some of the preposterous crashes you will see in the Middle East. It is quite good sport doing I-spy on some of the imaginative wrecks you will see. Think of it as an art form and hope to God you don't end up in one. You might as well anticipate a crash or two if you are doing much long-distance travel. There isn't much you can do about it. My own preferred option is to tranq out before I set out, either on *qat* in Yemen or on over-the-counter pharmaceuticals and booze everywhere else. On buses you will often be offered the front seat out of kindness. Up to you but in essence you are probably going to be pretty distracted by the sight of drivers watching videos (while they drive) and horrified by the number of near-misses you are going to see, rather than able to appreciate whatever scenery you are travelling through. About the middle of the bus is the best – the back three rows are cursed by perpetually open doors, bunches of trussed chickens and amplified bumps from the rear wheels.

A Long Ride in a Slow Machine

Trains: Tunisia and Morocco are the tops here, though the Cairo–Luxor run is enjoyable too. Trains feel safe and if you pay the extra money to travel first-class you get comfort and space – really the best way to travel, if you aren't pressed for time. Don't go third-class – it is full of backpackers whingeing and unpacking their rucksacks and shouting at the locals, who take it all in good part, handing live chickens round, hanging out of the empty window frames and generally just playing around. It can actually be quite a laugh occasionally going third-class but it gets boring unless you speak Arabic, and you have plenty time to meet these guys when the train stops for hours in the middle of nowhere, which they always do. Everyone unloads on the platform for a bit of shambling and shouting, stalls serving food appear from nowhere and well, what the heck, you're on holiday, think of it as a barbecue or something; there is no point getting ratty or even asking when the train will start moving again as no one will have the slightest idea.

Taxi

Obviously with taxi drivers, establish the price before you set off. In a nutshell, the plusher the taxi, the nearer the Hilton, the better the English spoken by the driver, the higher the fare. So you can either hang around for a real wreck, driven by some deranged shepherd on day-release with no command of any known language, and about as much right to be driving anything motorised as your cat has, or compromise. Second cheapest? Always a thought. All taxi drivers drive abominably, every taxi has a broken meter, lots of frilly things hanging from the windows and a few Koranic verses. The driving is the worst in Yemen. You have to recall that the national drug is a form of pretty powerful amphetamine, everyone chews it, no Yemeni has ever passed a driving test (or ever could), fear is unknown to them, and other cars are invisible. A scream a minute.

A Hitchhiker's Guide to the Middle East

Does not exist as such. If you flag a car or truck down, you will in general be expected to pay your way. In out-of-the-way places it is pretty much a rule as there is often no public transport. In this case it is vital to establish what you are expected to pay before you start. Going to Shahara in Yemen for example is extremely expensive but as it involves a four to six hour drive up a mountain it can be justified to a certain extent. Mostly public transport is what you will end up using, and it is pretty cheap. Women should not attempt to hitchhike, it is always misconstrued. Woman flagging down car = prostitute, in the Arab mind. This is a bit sad but it is better to know what is going through their minds when a car-load of sweating Egyptians beckons you towards their car.

The Arab
Archipelago

The Arab Archipelago runs from Morocco round to Yemen. One of the easiest and most informative ways of thinking of the Middle East is of a series of inhabited islands in a sea of sand, rubble and dryness. The size of individual countries gives no idea of population or more importantly how that population is distributed within the borders. Huge tracts of the Middle East are seriously uninhabitable, home to a few oases and nomads but not something you can effectively tie into a national framework, far less into a picture of a continuous swathe of inhabited territory running from the Atlantic to the Red Sea. Libya for example looks moderately huge on any map, but apart from the coastal strip it is virtually uninhabited.

More interesting is the fact that within many countries, where the population clusters in different areas and are separated by distance and poor terrain, entirely different cultures have developed. The most obvious of these are the Berbers in north Africa, who are physically and linguistically distinct from the strictly Arab populations which came in with the eighth-century conquests. By now the differences have been eroded and the remains of Berber culture as a separate entity are very limited. This stems from the fact that the Arab populations were often at odds if not actually at war with the Berber tribes and once they got the upper hand (by about the nineteenth century), a policy of discrimination and erasing Berber norms (and Berbers) got under way. The Berber villages which remain in the south of Tunisia or Algeria are sad, near-empty shells, most of the people who remain are the oldsters. The only people who come to visit are tourists. The young men are away in the nearest big town trying to earn a living. A dying culture, but one that used to flourish.

As so little land is usable, the distinction between town and country is much greater than in Europe. Bedouin is an over-used word not much thought about except in romantic Lawrence of Arabia terms in Europe, but to Arabs it is a crucial distinction. Town Arabs are quite as uneasy at the sight of a Bedouin camp as many European householders are at the sight of a gypsy camp. Bedouins by their nature have to be nomadic – the areas they inhabit are basically rubbish, barely livable in, and at times of the year conditions get so wretched that they have to decamp to the edges of the heavily settled areas. This is often where they trade in surplus camels (or these days quite as likely in smuggled cigarettes or arms). Town Arabs are insistent about the nobility of the Bedouin nomads and their traditions but keep a tight hold on their wallets while they are saying it.

These days the only 'nomads' you are likely to run into are scattered groups of rip-off artists hanging around Petra or the Sinai resorts, Wadi Ruum, that sort of place. They are now catering for the kind of fraudulent 'desert experience' which addles quite a lot of independent travellers' brains. Nomadic life is virtually extinct. These days camels are transported in the back of four-wheel-drive trucks, and they hardly make the grade as transport anywhere in the region any more.

A Pan-Arab Infrastructure?

This always looks like a good idea. Indeed the poor, populous bits of the Middle East are forever suggesting it to the rich, sandy bits. It doesn't look such a good idea to them. It'll be a long time before you get any Kuwaitis voting for a Baghdad–Kuwait motorway, and much the same length of time on a Cairo–Riyadh link. The rich Arab states are all in favour of immobility: the last thing they want is two million Egyptians on their doorstep claiming citizenship in the name of Arab brotherhood. This is the 'Turkeys don't vote for Christmas' school of politics.

Bad Lands

The simple picture of desert land as long sandy dunes stretching away in weird lunar patterns applies in some areas, parts of the Libyan desert for example, but a much higher percentage of the agriculturally useless land isn't so clear-cut, scrubby stony wastelands, mountains, stretches of what look like junk left over from a rubble-throwing competition, dried-out wadis. And the litter, no one mentions that. The burnt-out car wrecks, rusting oil drums, 100,000 Coke cans thrown from 100,000 car windows. Old fridges, you name it; on the face of it Bedouins seem to be the worst litter louts in the world.

FAR OUT

A few deranged pot-holes in the middle of the desert are inhabited. These are the sort of place that 'travellers' go to to commune with whatever it is that makes them think they are superior to your standard tourist slob. Most of the folk who live in, say, a Berber village, know they represent a dying culture. Dying out, frankly, for good reason. The customs have become irrelevant – this may be sad in many ways, but there is nothing you can do about it. It is genuinely a waste of time to try and encourage people to maintain customs they have themselves lost interest in. It is at best patronising and at worst dangerous.

Western liberals jump up and down and scream at the mention of female circumcision, but for some people that *is* a traditional custom, one thankfully dying out as the cranky elders get real. The theory, and a particularly contradictory one, is that they 'must' keep cute customs, weird clothes, exotic dances, photogenic festivals, things that thrill the sensation-seeking 'traveller' (never 'tourist'). Equally they 'must' stop infanticide, or child marriages or that part of the canon of local customs which is for whatever reason deemed undesirable by Western liberals. That, I believe, is called a logical argument. So how is that different from sitting in a four-star hotel watching a lot of guys doing the soft shoe shuffle in fezzes who later drive off in BMWs? At least the latter compromise means the guys get paid for fooling around, pretending to be dervishes, belly dancers or Bedouin nomads. Customs do die out, simple as that. You simply cannot force people to observe what you think are (or should be) their customs. New customs take their place, principally those of hassling liberal tourists for money, sex, etc. So you are adding to the problem. Just leave them in peace to get rid of customs or not as suits them.

These out-of-the-way places are normally pox-eaten holes. Nothing to eat, nothing to do. The only people you can talk to are feminist Danes conducting social research on these poor benighted bastards. The inhabitants of the area who have been dim enough to stay there are normally the sad remains of a dying culture. Up to you, go and visit them if you feel you must.

CIVIL WARS, LOCAL SQUABBLES, TRIBAL BIFF-OUTS

Conditions always vary from those described in any guide book. Things flare up, cool down and indeed remain much the same at times. The best suggestion is to take advice. This is not always freely offered. Clearly it is embarrassing for officials to admit parts of their country are temporarily no-go areas, but you may get an indication when permits to visit specific places become 'unavailable'. This can just be capricious, but it is worth wondering why it is suddenly 'impossible' to go to one area or another. It may be that some trouble or another has brewed up and, to ensure your safety, the kindly official has decided you'd better not go there. It can also be that he doesn't like the look of your face or genuinely finds it hard to believe that anyone in his right mind wants to go to an area he considers to be a shithole full of low-rent losers or any combination of the above. If you are going to obscure places, try and solicit advice on current conditions before you set off. Advice from locals should be completely ignored unless you know that the individual you are talking to actually comes from the area you are going to, in which case it may be true, or indeed may be an imaginative pack of lies.

If you are getting impatient and thinking: 'Well sod you Mr Guide book writer, the only way to find out is to go there,' yes, you are quite right. What worries me is what you might find when you get there, particularly if you are silly enough to travel unaccompanied by someone from the region. Local tax collection in parts of North Yemen can, for example, equal shooting you and taking your car. In more civilised Egypt, Assiyut may be described as 'uninteresting' by an official either because it genuinely is, or because this week they are doing a big security clampdown on the town, shooting up any fundamentalists they find. Interesting for budding Kate Adies. Decide for yourself of course, but if you have been systematically discouraged from going somewhere, go carefully. Warning signals are either an increase in frequency in checkpoints or an increase in the number of soldiers at checkpoints (pretty obvious really). Bad ones are when the uniforms change between one checkpoint and the next. This means one of two things: you are right in the middle of a civil war, or the checkpoint you are at is being manned by specialist forces who have been put in to do a bit of localised nastiness.

If you are shot at on approaching a checkpoint, it is tricky to know what to do. U-turn and hightail it back the way you came is the immediate reaction, but that may have been a warning shot meaning: 'Slow down, we are about to search you.' And so scarpering off up the road can get you into further, more serious trouble. I don't know in this situation – serves you right for not pulling out of your trip earlier is my gut reaction, as I can't think of a scrap of useful advice. I'd play it dumb and sweet and hope for the best: i.e. stop the car where you are (presumably out of effective range, or you'd be dead), and await developments, reserving your run-for-it option until last. And good luck even if you have been a bit silly getting yourself stuck in this particular position.

Well Die Then, See if I Care

Suicidal macho Europeans are forever taking on more than they can handle. Certainly if you are well prepared a lot of these gung-ho trips are at least survivable, but there exists a distinct sub-group of folk who decide to do such things more or less on a whim, rent a 4WD and drive off into the sunset. Off-road driving is not something you can learn on the job – the best thing that will happen is you write off the motor before you get too far from where you started. In order of stupidity here are a few 'Plans' which may not get you killed but, even if you are well organised, will get you pretty close.

Looking for the lost oases of the Sahara

Sort of self-explanatory this really. Nomadic tribes don't 'lose' oases – they either dry up or they become too difficult or dangerous to get to. Betting on boozers' luck to get you to places which may in fact not exist is frankly idiotic.

Going to visit obscure tribal configurations, visiting bizarre Bedouins, disputed border areas, etc., etc.

Often the reason you can't get a travel permit to such places is not 'the state' oppressing you. It is a lot more likely to be because the locals' sole means of generating income is robbing and at times murdering incomers. There are plenty of gush-eyed travel books written about these sorts of areas, but in general terms one may assume a certain amount of lying is going on. Note also, the number of books of this kind published give no indication of how many planned books fucked up at the first hurdle; that is, of surviving the experience. Normally you are safe enough if invited by a local resident who will be accompanying you. He'd lose a lot of face if you were killed while under his protection. However airheads do far too often decide to do this sort of thing off their own bats.

Unfortunately enough of them survive to trick other people into giving it a go.

Being the first person to hang-glide off somewhere remote

Fair enough, everyone in remote places is armed and the temptation to shoot at something large, brightly coloured and unfamiliar floating around the sky is unlikely to be resisted for long. It can get to be a bit of a drag shooting crows.

Hiking

Yemen is the place for this, if you are pretty rugged and really into your hardship. There are villages out there which haven't seen a hiker before and others which have seen plenty and buried them all in the wadi. It is therefore essential to ask advice from the expatriate community before setting off. There will be folk hanging around who do this kind of thing. The Atlas Mountains in north Africa and Wadi Rum in Jordan are other hiking favourites. Any kind of long hike should be planned very carefully and not undertaken if you aren't right into this kind of recreation. You should definitely leave your planned itinerary with someone responsible, possibly at the embassy. Unforeseen disasters are just that and if no one knows even approximately where you are, you will be in deep trouble.

Small Scale Maps

Not something you are allowed to possess in many countries and lone foreigners wandering around out-of-the-way places with maps are regarded with extreme suspicion by officials. Arabs never do this kind of thing and the only motivation they ascribe to it is spying, so you can get into all sorts of tedious nonsense with the local policemen who have not normally been sent to do their tour of duty in 'GibberGoat' because of their blinding intelligence and promotion prospects.

Camping

This is very difficult to explain to anyone who comes across you. Cops regard people sleeping out as in some way a bad thing: they may suspect that you have some dodgy agenda, sneaking up and peeking through the wire of army camps, that kind of thing, and treat you with hostility. Also there are no campsites and pitching your tent in the middle of nowhere can get you attention from packs of wild and occasionally rabid dogs. If you are into wadi-walking or hill-climbing you will know what kind of kit you need if you are sleeping out miles from anywhere, and the only additional recommendation is to take a really substantial quantity of water. Equally important is to take water in containers that won't rupture. The five-litre plastic 'jerry cans' available throughout the region don't rupture. The 1.5-litre bottles do. The five-litre size normally require a deposit.

Desert Trekking

Horrible places really, deserts, but some people claim to enjoy the experience of desert travelling. Go with an organised and sensible group if you want to do such things. And stick to 4WD treks. Arabs are sensible and if they have jacked in the camel, it is for a good reason. Nothing short of being soft in the head should induce you to undertake camel trekking in the desert. No Arab would do it from choice, the cost is astronomical for a long trek and the discomforts are reputed to be spectacular. If there is a nastier natured animal than the camel, I'll be very surprised. They are genuinely horrible beasts, forever trying to bite you, crapping all over the place and moaning their ugly faces off from dawn to dusk. Not an animal you want hanging around. The key word is 'organised' if you are considering this form of recreation. It is simply suicidal to round up a car, a few mates and a six-pack and head off into the desert.

Trekking is a know-your-dealer exercise, in spades. You are going to be putting yourself in the hands of a man you don't know for several days in wretched conditions. Some of these guys are utter bastards, and are quite happy spending all the daylight hours trying to squeeze more money out of you. Once you are a day out, you are absolutely sunk if the 'Hey Man you can trust me' Arab guide turns out to be as above. You can't even murder him and escape because you don't know the way back. Also note, just because someone dresses like a Bedouin it doesn't necessarily mean he is one. City boys wanting to turn a profit hire gear and camels and lead off parties of tourists. So what can happen is you are heading off with some townie in fancy dress who knows about as much about camels as you do and whose idea of where you are going boils down to 'yonder'.

A Bike

For the suicidally inclined, mountain bike trekking is an as yet untried phenomenon in the Middle East. There are treks organised to Morocco: the High Atlas Mountains contain an enormous number of treacherous goat tracks, spectacular vistas and satisfyingly long drops to a grisly death for the unprepared bike traveller. Do not even *think* about this form of recreation unless you are experienced (very), fit (very), and have no living dependants who give a shit about you.

The organised treks start from Imlil but of course the benefits of any kind of trekking are spoiled if the place is full of French mountain bikers. You should prepare very carefully for this kind of holiday. Going in a group of less than three is short-sighted, as any accident will involve on-the-hoof repairs, and any injury will involve you extracting yourself plus crippled friend from a trackless mountain range in the middle of nowhere. The locals are pretty cool in the High Atlas but they will (quite justifiably) consider you to be a total nut job, if you come cycling over the local mountain pass. I suppose it would be theoretically possible to try this sort of thing in Yemen – the mountains are absolutely spectacular, going up to 3,200 metres and half the country is off-road terrain. If you cycle into a Yemeni village that is not on the local road network the locals' first reaction would be to shoot you, unless they got the giggles at the sheer spectacle first. Give it a try, why don't you?

Out of Sight

There are a great number of places in the Middle East which are very time-consuming and difficult to get to. As you travel round of course you will meet people who will recommend such places. Do notice that no one ever admits they've spent three days' hard travel and nearly a hundred quid to get to what turns out to be a dull shitbox in the middle of nowhere, which must happen sometimes, by the law of averages if nothing else. The usual get-out clause in this case is to claim that they have 'received some deep insight from the way these people live their lives'. What you will normally learn is that these people are bored out of their minds, sunk in squalor, and the best you can say about them is that they *are* abandoning their traditional customs.

SNAPSHOT: DONKEY RIDE
TO VALLEY OF KINGS

Are you over four foot eight? Do you know how big donkeys are? Do you have a labrador? If you can answer YES! to all of the above, you are in a position to assess the extent to which you will enjoy this form of holiday recreation.

1) Straddle labrador
2) Go 'Giddyup'
3) See how much fun it is walking into the town centre with labrador clamped between your knees.

Of course things are much different in Luxor – everyone wants to sell you on this, so it must be great eh? It *is* different from your family pet experiment. Here the donkeys climb up mountains (see 3 above), it is about 130°F, the water you have thoughtfully brought with you has either run out, or the bottle has sprung a leak when your donkey has decided to do something energetic, or you foolishly believed your guide when he claimed that water was available at moderate cost at his uncle's/cousin's/etc. house. Ten dollars for a bottle of water, welcome to Egypt.

Your friendly and fluent guide will prove rapacious in the most unexpected manner. He will arbitrarily decide to stop for cocktails at some four-star concrete box growing out of the boiled landscape. He will prove sickly, claiming he can't make it to the sights you have paid for. He will become elvish, poking his stick up your donkey's arse when you have managed to stop the wretched thing after one of the headlong darts which seem to be the only form of locomotion donkeys are really capable of. He will wax philosophic on such matters as the unimportance of money and your inability to navigate home from the trackless waste if he decided to run off in a fit of spontaneity. He will confide in you, share his knowledge of English, 'Mein Herr, Baksheesh, good.' If necessary he will tell you mangled lies about unobtrusive tumuli while infant relatives attempt to convince you that the ancient Egyptians bought their grave ornaments from twentieth-century Taiwan. Surreal ain't it? But, the next morning, was it worth it? You bet, if your idea of a happy waking is feeling as if you've been imaginatively buggered by the Rumanian secret police.

Lonesome Sights

If you are visiting very isolated monuments or out-of-the-way tombs, be careful. They are sometimes inhabited by bats or rabid dogs. These can scare the living shit out of you so take a torch and carry a stick if you are poking into tombs, don't just blunder in. Equally some such places are inhabited by families of impoverished locals, in which case go easy on the torch and stick approach. If nothing else, having a foreigner appearing in your living room doing a pasty-faced imitation of Indiana Jones is a bit embarrassing all round.

SITES IN THE MIDDLE EAST FALL INTO TWO CATEGORIES

1) Far too easy for anyone to get to. These are coach-partied to bits, full of rip-off artists and half-starved camels which you will have whipped under your nose by men shouting, 'Mister you want camel ride, me good man, take AMEX.' That kind of place.

2) Far too bloody difficult to get to. These are beloved of really the worst sort of travel snob, he who says, 'I vas ze second man to hang-glide off zis wonderful tomb. Now it is only the tourists who come here. They do not understand the simple life of zese people.'

Good and double good if you are jumping up and screaming, 'I've met that bastard!', but even so, many out-of-the-way sites are more than worth a look. There is something disheartening about being stuck in a 'popular' tomb with a tour group of pensioners. However it is often difficult and expensive to get to any other places, and guide books aren't always that helpful, often having been written by people who have never been anywhere near the places they so lovingly describe.

Egypt and Turkey in particular have so many interesting and varied places that no two-week tourist can do much more than take in the motorway sites. Anything even a couple of notches off the beaten track is worth a try. Probably the best bet is to compromise, and to balance the amount of time you have against the obscurity of the places you plan to visit. Travelling for days to get to an unexplored desert fort is a bit like Russian roulette. The longer it takes, the worse the position you are in if you arrive and think, 'Well this is pretty dismal.' If you've just travelled for twenty-four hours, obviously you can't just say, 'Fuck it' and get the first return trip. It is sensible to have a fall-back attraction in the vicinity to go and stay in, if the first turns out not to be to your taste and, even more sensible, to make sure that you can leave when you choose, not when the only taxi in town is full enough to warrant moving. Another possibility is to set yourself a time limit. Myself I use three hours, that is I don't go *anywhere* that is more than three hours' drive from a half-decent bar. This gives you time to get back the same day if the place you have visited is not up to much. The horror of travelling for twenty-four hours to find that not only are you visiting a decaying pile of mud with windows, but that there isn't a drink of anything and the locals' sole form of recreation is stoning the foreigners and shouting, 'Korean' or even 'Roman' after you in the street. Never again. Three hours' drive from a bar *max*.

Getting Trapped

This follows from the going-to-obscure-places syndrome. If you have chartered a shared taxi to get there, or otherwise had to organise your own transport, there is absolutely no guarantee that anyone will be leaving the place in the foreseeable future. If the lift you have organised involves a family going home and taking you as a passenger, you might have to wait until someone else fancies leaving Wadi Dung. Waiting for a lift on the way out you are a completely captive audience and everyone knows it: the driver can ask whatever price he damn well pleases and after an unplanned week stuck in an obscure and tedious village, you'll pay it with pleasure.

Crumbling Monuments

Most famous of these is the Sphinx, which is really in a terrible state – being awarded the job of preserving the Sphinx is the equivalent of leaving a loaded revolver on an unpopular minister's desk. One option is patching it up, which is impossible as the thing is made out of rotten rock and sucks water up from the ground like a sponge. The alternative is to rebuild it, à la Disney. Both courses are political suicide. Maintenance of ruins is really of greater importance to foreigners than to locals, who have plenty of their own problems and not much money. The preferred option is to repaint the most popular sites, so the Valley of Kings is getting new friezes drawn on to make the paintings more closely resemble the horrible souvenirs on sale outside. The area is so full of ruins that important sites are neglected, knocked down, rebuilt or just ignored except as a source of building materials.

Slumberland

Slum junkies who want to go and wring their hands at real squalor should be barred anyway. Unless you have a professional or social reason for visiting any of the really fucked-out bits of Cairo, just don't. It is demeaning both to them and to you. Dar Al Labnan would do you as a location if you want to disregard advice and preach liberal rubbish about how friendly 'the poor and oppressed are' when you get home. The edges of Fustan are pretty manky as well. I hope the locals slit your throats if you go there to take 'sensitive/patronising' photos. How anyone can actually stand living in such places escapes me. That they manage to do so with dignity is impressive.

MIGRATION

The parts of any big Arab city you don't see are the 'Biladiya' sections – barely coherent slums, without water or electricity, which rural populations migrate to. You will rarely see shanty towns, but they exist out of your sight. Some are delineated by the trades practised in them, thus you will get slaughtering quarters, rubbish tips, rag-pickers, all congregated in separate areas carrying out one particular function. Some, normally socially more cohesive and respectable, are based round people from one part of the country. They tend to stick together and to replicate the rural society they have left against the backdrop of the cities. These areas can be quite intriguing and are safe to visit if you are specifically invited.

One interesting aspect of these Biladiya areas is how successfully they manage to mirror village life. The city itself seems to disappear and most of the people living in the quarter rarely leave it. The whole model is one of self-contained poverty with livestock and exchange of labour being the general currency. A minority of the men may work in the public parts of the city, some indeed may have relatively respectable jobs – lift attendants, waiters, etc., but still they prefer to live in an area where they are known and they know the rules. The whole system operates on a sliding scale of niceties – there is always someone these people can look down on, someone who is poorer, more immoral or whatever.

This retention of village life in the city and the city's lack of interest in the inhabitants often means that there are no services, electrics or water. Sometimes the Islamic charities will run a small clinic or a primary school. They can operate as Islam is a recognised feature of village life, whereas central government is not. An easy impression to take away, and one which Westerners habitually do, is that these areas are 'hotbeds of Fundamentalism'. Not really the case. The generally conservative morés are village ones and Islam is much more a solace than some political rallying cry. The influence of Islamic organisations is generally beneficial, and a lot of the hostility you might occasionally get is based on the fact that these folk earn less in a year than you spend on a pair of trousers. Undoubtedly more poor than rich people join the Islamic movements, but this seems logical enough as these are the only organisations which make an appearance out in these areas and the community of Islam is one way of compensating for the deep sense of rootlessness which these migrants feel, far from the land that they generally miss terribly. To you their village may be some fuck-pot in the boonies. To them it was home and however well they fake the village community in the city they still feel the loss acutely.

If you are just wandering about town anyway and you stumble into an area where you are treated as an intrusion, back off. Poor people aren't necessarily over the moon at being photographed by bleeding-heart liberals and if you don't speak particularly good Arabic you can get stuck in situations which can appear threatening and at worst can actually be so. This is much more likely to happen in the trade-based enclaves than in the transplanted rural community areas, but it is often very difficult to tell which you are in. The rag-pickers or whoever are often outcasts from their own rural sub-communities and may therefore be less inclined to follow a conservative village-based reaction to your sudden appearance. In general, stay clear of these communities unless invited. As much as anything else because you genuinely won't know what the rules are and being there without a reason might require in itself some explanation.

Refugee Camps

Don't go to these unless invited. Displaced Palestinians are very hospitable so you may well be given an invitation, but turning up uninvited to poke around is a real no-no. Refugee camps are not tent cities, indeed some of them are indistinguishable from residential areas and successful Palestinians often remain. in the camps long after they could afford to move to a more affluent suburb, as a show of national solidarity. Strangers are inevitably viewed with suspicion: a certain amount of military training goes on in some of the camps and they are always very political in outlook. Palestinian refugees know that they have been massacred in these camps rather too often and an uninvited stranger asking about the layout of the camp may easily be mistaken for some spook casing the joint.

THE KURDS

The Kurds are a mountain people – they form a substantial minority of the population of Iraq, Iran and Turkey and are a thorough nuisance to all of them. The Kurds even by Middle Eastern standards are a hotheaded bunch. If they are not being invaded or terrorised by their neighbours, they get bored and start fighting each other. If Kurdistan ever achieved independence the odds are extremely high that we would see the world's first instance of Auto-Genocide. Divided isn't in it. Inside the Arab countries with substantial Kurdish minorities Kurds tend to be viewed in much the same way as Russians regard Chechens in Moscow, and for very similar reasons. Kurds tend to hang out together and are often involved in criminal or semi-criminal activities. Thus for example the tourist business in Turkey is increasingly Kurdish-controlled.

The Turkish Kurds are the most numerous, and the most systematically oppressed. There has, in effect, been an undeclared war of assimilation/extermination going on in south-east Turkey for the last fifty-odd years. The Kurdish language was banned until very recently and a policy of discrimination, imprisonment and 'police actions' is more or less the Turkish government's policy. Iraqi and Iranian Kurds tend to be used as political pawns in the quarrels between the two countries. That is, Iran backs

Iraqi Kurds (or some of them) and suppresses its own. Iraq backs Iranian Kurdish factions and really whacks around its own. The massacre at Halabja in 1988 where poison gas was used against the Kurds is one example of Iraqi 'policy' towards the Kurds within its own boundaries. Just to complicate matters further, Turkey has arrogated the right to pursue Kurdish fighters into northern Iraq. These deep border incursions would normally have provoked serious trouble between Iraq and Turkey but Iraq is still under the international cosh and has to put up with this.

Some squabble is building up here and as usual the Kurds will end up being the meat in the sandwich. America is thinking about sticking its nose in, but no outsider has ever enjoyed interfering in the mare's nest of internal Kurdish politics and it would be a mistake to think that they can be sorted out from Washington.

Turkish Baths

The Arabic for these is *hammam* and they are some of the nicest places in the Middle East. It is as well to start in one that has seen tourists before. If at all possible you should go with an Arab acquaintance of the same sex. He or she will know the ropes with regard to local morés on modesty and how to behave once inside. Couples should never believe Arab guys who claim these baths are mixed. Don't even think about it unless you are both frustrated peepshow artistes. Baths, even in liberal countries, are strictly segregated. Women's hours tend to be in the morning, but check. One favourite trick to pull on Western women is to say, 'It is no problem, lady, in you go, really, they are mixed.' And just wait for that awful moment when you get your kit off and walk into a room full of over-heated Arab men who are seeing more of you than they have ever seen of their wives . . .

Ignoble Savages: We Shall Fight Each Other on the Beaches

You begin to get the drift at the check-in at Manchester airport. You hear the hum of odd dialects. Sixty-year-old women clutching bottles of rum and six-packs of Old Holborn sit on plastic bucket-seats. Groups of young men (earrings, tattoos, cut off t-shirts, 'Fuck you, mate' eyes) stand menacingly at the bar, and women (enormous wheelie-bin of a suitcase, short skirt, high heels and a heap of hair that looks like badly burnt candy floss) totter around the duty-free shops. At the check-in desk these folk behave exactly like proud but savage Bantus confronted by a miracle of technology – notice the way their eyes follow the luggage through that little hole in the wall, suspicion mingling with a sort of primitive awe. Who are they? you wonder. Where are they going? Then the penny drops, we are exporting these idiots to Turkey.

Half-way across the Med and you are already feeling a bit sorry for the Turks: singalongs, trouser dropping and the sort of dog-brained drunkenness unacceptable anywhere larger than a disused mining village are taking over. Mob tourism has come to south Turkey, dug itself in on the beaches, and is having itself a whale of a time. When the Turks come to think of it, they preferred Gallipoli – at least there they got to shoot the invaders. Talk with the Turks twenty kilometres back from the coast and you will find they are in shock, with the same thousand-yard stare of soldiers who saw something horrid in Vietnam. Maybe undercutting Majorca was a mistake after all. The Turks thought, sensibly enough, that encouraging tourism was a good way of earning foreign currency. What they didn't fully appreciate was that Britain and most of north Europe actually contains people who 'enjoy' themselves to destruction on holiday. Fighting, fucking in public, drinking yourself unconscious in 45-degree heat all seems a bit, well, scummy, to Turks. So be sensitive with the guys who have been working on the coast – when they find out you are British they can't talk to you without expecting you to suddenly vomit on them or drop your trousers. Coax them into seeing you as a bit more human, it's worth the effort.

It's a puzzle to the Turks – 'Who are these people? Is Britain dumping its prison population on Turkish beaches? What is going on here? Britain doesn't exactly have an image problem with Turks, it's just that the image they have of Britain as rather a staid and civilised society doesn't in the least square with the people who go there for two-week breaks. They are seeking some explanation and there really isn't anything you can say.

'Yes, people this ignorant do exist, sorry about that Mehmet old boy,' is about as near as you can get, but the problem still worries them.

'Do they behave like this all the time?'

'No, they save up their money all year and come and spend two weeks here in a drunken stupor, fighting each other or fucking equally drunk young ladies who take their fancy. It is called a holiday.'

'But . . .'

'The burning of skin to an unhealthy red and the wearing of peculiar leisurewear, it is the tradition.'

By this stage you are sweating a bit yourself. It does look pretty thin on paper.

You have to have a pretty ropey economy to put up with this sort of invasion. Any well-off country would simply seal and then bomb the beaches, and forget about issuing brochures for next year. Maybe it's better to keep them corralled in a relatively small part of the country than let them roam free. When you get away from the coast things start going in the right direction, prices drop (beer halves in price away from the tourist resorts), and Turkey turns into a country rather than some hell-on-earth tourist theme park. The first time you cup hands to receive a dash of eau de cologne before the bus starts you realise this is bus heaven. Turkey is huge and travelling can take forever but the bus journeys are so cunningly constructed that, just as the journey is starting to get on your nerves, the bus stops for ten minutes at a roadside rest, you stretch, disembark, get a snack or a glass of sugary pop, wander around a bit and get back on the bus refreshed and ready to do it all again. There is always something to see – your eyes catch details as you flick past, rusty advertisements for banks, mountains, a castle or two, concrete irrigation systems, batty little kids with their heads shaved to the bone doing cartwheels at the side of the road. Some are trying to stop the traffic to sell flowers or jars of honey or whatever is produced locally.

Free enterprise has run wild in the Turkish transport system –

there are thousands of buses going everywhere. The Turks used to be nomads, maybe they still get the urge. The standard of driving dips as you go east and by the time you reach the Syrian border the drivers are beginning to get a bit madder, the number of near-misses pick up, but by that stage you are hypnotised and it doesn't seem to matter. You are a thousand miles from the beach bums, and who can blame you. The Turkish guy in the next seat smiles, offers you a cigarette or a couple of tangerines – he knows it too.

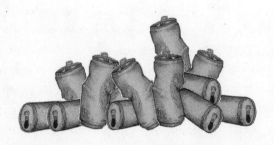

Binges

If you do decide to go on an all-day drink until you drop number, don't do it in the sun. There is nothing easier than getting semi-lethal sunburn which can knock four or five days out of any holiday and if you get sunstroke it can be near fatal. Choose your location, make it at least shady and, unless you are a real leather skin, cover the back of your neck. You dehydrate faster than you do in Britain so to maximise the time and amount you can drink, use ice water as a chaser. Nearly all drunken behaviour causes grave offence in the Middle East – just because the waiter continues to serve you, that doesn't mean he doesn't absolutely despise you for getting pissed. Nothing you can do about that, but some behavioural things can provoke violent trouble. So observe a few niceties.

All-male Groups

Shouting and fighting. Yeah well, in resorts these might be tolerated, though you can get yourself well hated. Fighting with locals is a no-no – that and hassling local women should be crossed off the list however soused you get. These are both murdering offences and even if you are all fit as butchers' dogs you are very outnumbered. Arabs work on a much longer fuse than Europeans but once it burns out you are all fair game. By this stage, even in tourist resorts, this sort of behaviour can be a police/soldier matter. If things get to the stage where one of your number seems about to be dragged off to the pokey, either back down in spades or make a break for the tourist compound you came from. Don't get banged up in the Middle East.

Any of the above behaviour (including getting drunk) is out of the question in areas not used to tourists.

Mixed Groups

Don't fuck in public anytime, anyplace, anywhere.

Spirit Binges

In countries where beer isn't readily available, the odds are you will binge on spirits either with local low-life or expatriates. Since expatriate measures are typically half a pint of whisky with an ice cube floating on top, it is sensible to be drinking water on the side, lots of it. You can lose about half your body weight after chug-a-lugging a litre of neat whisky. Also, with spirits you go from nought to sixty in about three seconds, that is you get howling, barking drunk in less time than seems conceivable. You get arrested on the way home or fall asleep in the street and get bitten by local (rabid?) dogs. You go nuts and kick the windows of your hostess's house in. Quite entertaining in short, but if you don't keep a pint glass of water running through your system at the same time, you will experience the sort of hangovers that make you long for being bitten by a rabid dog.

POT NOODLES

Morocco, Turkey and the resorts in Sinai get the highest percentage of stoners and this little advice section is just for you.

You can get any type of drugs you fancy in the Middle East. One popular form of small-business enterprise in the region is to sell dope to foreign devils, shop them to the police, get a reward, get their dope back and start the process all over again. It is therefore essential when you are buying drugs in the Middle East from someone you don't know well that he doesn't find out where you are staying. This is easy enough in a big town like Cairo or Istanbul, but in small places everyone knows where individual foreigners are staying. Treat with a great degree of distrust people who approach you in the street and offer to sell you drugs – especially the case in Morocco. You will be much safer if you choose the Arab you want to approach, after a bit of consideration. Sound him out over a couple of cups of tea before bringing up the subject of *kif* (hashish). Street dealers are adept at ripping off tourists. Someone whose first use of English is something along the lines of, 'Hey man, you want to buy some hash?' is pretty sure he is going to make a substantial profit on the deal. Also (God – archive memorial advice) don't buy any form of drugs anywhere near Sultan Ahmet Square in Istanbul.

One more little watchword. Don't smoke with dealers in the Middle East. Well, do if you want, but at the very least be prepared for a real head fuck of a smoke. He does know about other drugs, so lucky you, you've just drunk a cup of tea with twenty tabs dissolved in it, you are sitting in a room with five lust-crazed dealers and you are: male/female/under 130 years old/not a household pet . . . If the tea tastes peculiar, or you start to feel something heavy-duty coming on, leave immediately. If you do get away after having been slipped some kind of chemical cocktail, you are very vulnerable to a real edge-of-the-seat holiday paranoia experience. Unexpected doses of LSD can really put the shits up you. Best bet is either to get back to your hotel and hope you can sleep the worst of it off – everything in the Middle East seems impossibly threatening or just odd if you're tripping. If you are more robust and have some experience with 'lucies try and get a six-pack down your neck before you crash out. It makes for a softer landing, and if you start enjoying yourself, by no means impossible, just carry on drinking, it all flattens out eventually. The other common nasty trick dealers play is to load the tea with downers, in the hope that you'll doze off and give them a chance to investigate your soft orifices. In this case don't mix in booze after you escape their clutches (if you do), rather get a cab back to your hotel and sleep it off. Cab rather than walk because these sorts of doses can lead to you falling over in the street.

Quality Control

You *can* get excellent quality hash, sometimes too good. Some of the Riif specials in Morocco are pretty heavy going. You can also get sold rubbish hennaed lumps of dope. Depends what you smoke at home. If you are still at the soap bar/cooking hash stage, go carefully with some of the GTX hashes on offer, they can be a lot more vivid and spacy than you are used to.

Drug Binges

These tend, particularly in Morocco, to be the old interface between you and local Arabs. People's motivation for filling you full of expensive hash may not be entirely altruistic (what a surprise). You may well be expected to pony up with some form of sexual favour. Also, Moroccans are adept at putting the hex on your relaxing vision of the great eternity or whatever. Do as you like of course, but the ones to be watchful of are going to some house in the middle of nowhere for a smoke. This seems obvious, but if you are driven out somewhere for a smoke it can seem perfectly plausible and the fact that your journey back in one piece was never guaranteed will not be emphasised by your host. This particularly applies to 'offers' to go for a smoke in the farms around Ketama in Morocco. In this situation, a surprise tab of acid in your tea can be an utter disaster, even if you escape having your bodice ripped off. You can find yourself ten miles from nowhere experiencing a genuine plutonium-enriched hit of the, 'Oh God! the stars are getting real close' nature, stuck on your own in the middle of a field with sex-starved Moroccans fanning out around you with their fake Ronsons crooning, 'White wo/man jig a jig jig, jig a jig!'

Could possibly induce a touch of paranoia.

Green Revolution

As mentioned before, the Yemenis have an all new, guaranteed, bay-at-the-moon-in-public, nightmare hit. *Qat*. This has become a club drug over the last few years but in Britain the quantities taken are minuscule. In Yemen it is practically the basis of society.

It is a difficult drug to take, but rewarding. What you buy is a bush of what looks like privet hedge, which you chew, swallowing the juice produced. It is painful at first and may cause your gums to bleed. Worth persisting with, as this is the only way to meet Yemenis and the effects are just excellent – completely variable as well, you never quite know what sort of mood it will put you in. Anything from mild hallucinations to speedy hits to stoner loquacity. A great drug really. It's particularly useful for travelling as it irons out the discomforts and stops you worrying about the disgracefully low standards of driving. It also makes Yemenis pleased, to see a foreigner indulging in the national vice. It is, however, important for Westerners to make sure if they are chewing and travelling that they have a copious supply of water – bits of the leaves do get wedged in the throat and you develop a hell of a thirst. Also the taste, till you get used to it, is vile. So it is worth investing in a couple of bottles of Coca-Cola, which takes the taste away very effectively. It would be a waste of time to go to Yemen and not chew *qat*, it's just the cherry on the cake for an already insane destination to spend as much of your time as is possible out of your face on an organic, legal and weird social drug. Don't miss out. This also explains why driving in Yemen is so absolutely unbelievably awful, even by Middle Eastern standards, as everyone is completely whacked out on a cocktail of speed and LSD while they drive. Great! A crackerjack idea.

Smack Binges

Only for the really dedicated. This isn't acceptable behaviour anywhere in the Middle East and your neighbours will shop you if you are cooking up a storm on the premises, and they will spot you, don't worry about that. At least if you are caught you shouldn't have to worry about being sent to jail. You might have to worry about being hanged or beheaded though. The penalties for a touch of chemicals would bring a tear to Michael Howard's eye. Up to you as ever. This having been said, the quality is rumoured to be excellent. Really heroin is not a holiday option and if you don't have the option of not taking it, you probably don't have enough money to go on holiday.

Drug Smuggling

Do not try to pay for your holiday by doing this. On a purely practical level you may get ripped off at source. The sheer embarrassment of a man who has smuggled two kilos of henna back into the country is a pleasure to see. If you check the haggling section (see p.149) you will see that you will not get a good deal from any Arab – they can always outwit you. Good for them, but when it comes to major (and illegal) purchases you can't exactly complain if the goods turn out to be not as advertised.

Still keen? God some clucks are reading this book. Another 'way' of doing this is to act as a courier for someone else. Naivety personified, an informer will shop you. The dealer gets his hash back, the police get some of their credibility back, you get locked in the pokey until hell freezes over.

Jailhouse Rock

Time in Arab prisons is to be avoided (see above section). If you do get sentenced to five years in a Moroccan jail you will have a pretty grim time and there is no guarantee you'll get a film made of your experiences. At the very least you'll be bored to the edge of madness by having as your only company for five years a German hippie whose brain has ossified at about 1973. And I'm afraid if you have a cute white butt, you probably won't by the time you leave. I leave the details to your imagination.

Sentence Construction

First things first, drugs are widely consumed everywhere in the Middle East.

Sentences for any form of involvement with drugs range from

the punitive to the fatal. It does happen you know – particularly in stoner resorts, there seems such a free and easy atmosphere that you get sloppy, smoke in public and then there is a clampdown and bingo, looks like your two-week holiday is going to have a five-year extension tacked on to it. This is just for dope offences – if you are doing chemicals and get caught, it's sweet goodbye to you. Foreigners never get a fair trial in the Middle East (don't get paranoid, neither do locals unless they 'know' someone, in which case they don't get any trial at all). So put all this together and what do you get? A choice between five years in the pokey and getting economically and peacefully out of your face. Know your dealer is very much the rule.

Paybacks

BIG BIZARRES

These are the tourist-processing bazaars of the Middle East where many people end up trying to buy souvenirs. High-pressure salesmanship and lots of spotters grabbing you by the arm and steering you into shops which sell nasty over-priced rubbish. Don't however get all snooty and avoid the big bazaars. They started out as areas that sold things to locals and, if you shop around, a few old-fashioned shops exist selling weird but desirable odds and ends. Even the Grand Bazaar in Istanbul, which is little more than a shopping mall selling tawdry souvenirs, is worth wandering around as out-of-the-way shops not entirely geared to tourists still exist, selling the most peculiar bits and pieces. In general the nearer you get to the fringes of any big market, the more interesting the items on sale become. Local merchandise has often been driven out of the central historical core of the bazaar, but is still on sale in the surrounding streets.

You will not get a bargain in any shop that is selling souvenirs: i.e. mostly carpets, leather, brass or alabaster. Any shop that belongs to 'My friend/My brother' should be treated with intense suspicion as you are chaperoned into its jaws by the guy you have 'bumped into' five minutes before. You'll drop the most money if you start buying unhallmarked gold, 'precious' stones, 'perfumes' or carpets. The trouble is that Arab salesmen have got your psychology sorted out in spades. 'No, no, you buy nothing, is no problem, only look,' he says. But, after you've drunk fifteen cups of tea and been shown two hundred carpets 'only to look', the old resistance does begin to suffer and, out of politeness, you make some more or less favourable comment on one rug or another. Leads to a sticky end – you are absolutely doomed if you believe you can out-haggle any Arab. You can't. It is impossible for any European to get an advantageous deal from an Arab, though painfully many claim to have done so. The best you can hope for is to reduce the price to something approximating the degree to which he would overcharge his neighbour. If you bear this in mind, haggling can be moderately entertaining. Just make sure you never end up trying to buy something you genuinely want – that stuffs you from the word go and don't think the beady-eyed vendor won't notice if you are seriously interested.

Everyone has his own theory on how to haggle. As none of them work, here's another one. Time-wasting is the key, though you are up against the experts. Ask politically insensitive questions, ask about local wheat production, talk about anything apart from the piece you expect to be able to buy. Go across to other shops, buy teas for beggars, generally be a waste of space and time. Just drivel on and you will discourage other tourists from coming into his shop. The vendor gets a bit jumpy and reduces the price. Carry on and repeat the whole procedure even more slowly if you can be bothered. Another possible ploy is to take a break. Say you will come back and then do so. Especially effective while he is closing a big deal with someone else. You'll still end up dropping money but driving the poor man half mad and boring him to death often means you get offered a 'piss off, loser' price which is reasonably near what a local might get. And it does take time, lots and lots of it. The key is boring the man til he fears he is losing trade and that you will come back day after day and louse up more lucrative deals. Don't worry about being heartless, he will always make a good profit from you however low you can get the price.

Don't believe the prices other tourists tell you they have got. Particularly mean Europeans, who get so distraught at the thought that they have paid too much that they habitually lie and claim to have bought living-room-sized antique carpets for fifty pence. They haven't, they are lying.

The Souks (This Sooks)

If you are reading this before you take your first holiday to the Middle East, ask yourself a few questions. Have you ever felt the slightest urge to buy a badly made nightdress? Curly-toed felt slippers, with lovely gold braid? Crudely woven mats in fluorescent colours? Ugly and impractical pieces of brasswork? Purple 'shrink to fit' leather jackets? You will. It must be something about the Middle East, but you end up coveting ridiculous items which, even when you bust your budget buying them, will go straight into your darkest cupboard when you get home. Retain a bit of perspective, avoid the hypnotised purchase of things which are basically shoddy and over-priced. Your friends will laugh when you get home, and once the fog clears from your head, you will wonder why indeed did you buy a three-foot-high brass hubble bubble pipe of almost startling tackiness?

Arabs are, however, the world's greatest salesmen. If you look at it logically, haggling is a great idea for snaring dummies – like the national lottery, everyone believes that somehow 'they' will be the one who buys 'The Greatest Bargain Ever Sold'. This is sound marketing on the Arab trader's part. No one can believe that *they* will be ripped off, and everyone knows they have the key to getting a real bargain. Eavesdrop on a tour group explaining how they got things reduced in price and that they all got a splendid deal, then think about it. Is it even marginally likely that Arab traders are so stupid that they have sold half the contents of their shop at a loss? The trick is of course to make you feel good about being robbed blind to buy something you didn't particularly want which will hang around your house for years like an albatross once you get back. Anyone dragging you into a shop is obviously doing this not just because he expects to lose money, but also because he is so overjoyed at being browbeaten by the master race that it is a privilege to sell you his tawdry stock at less than he paid for it. 'So what if the boss sacks me?' he reasons. 'At least the joy of being outwitted by a fat pensioner in Hawaiian shorts from Barnsley will teach me much about how to conduct my business in future.'

That's how they think . . . honest.

Ahh. That Urge to Buy Heavy Pieces of Ethnic Junk When You Are Miles from Anywhere

You've no idea what insane bits of rubbish will suddenly seem intensely desirable when you are in Bugaboo. Donkey saddles, baskets, repellent clay pots, all those cumbersome (though cheap) bits of the rich tapestry that makes up oasis life. Don't bother, even discounting the sheer difficulty of travelling onwards saddled with a ten-kilo mud pot or a crudely woven basket with a diameter of a metre and a half – these things just look dippy once you get them home.

Rip-offs

No enormous point going into all of these.

Perfume in Cairo. Stoned dummies for some reason actually believe some shifty little screwball is going to make them a fortune selling them perfume which they can then take to Israel and sell at enormous profit. Do you believe this when you see it in print? Does it even seem likely? Much the same applies to any special offer anyone seems determined to sell you in relatively fluent English. As soon as it is hinted that you are going to make a profit reselling whatever is being offered, you can be absolutely certain that you are about to be ripped off.

Carpet Tax

Think twice about that carpet.

> Tiny little fingers, tiny little toes:
> is how the hand-knotted carpet grows.

Funny though, plenty people who wouldn't consider hanging a tiger skin in their Islington flat somehow square the circle and buy themselves a hand-made carpet.

Just for the record you are almost certainly doing more harm than you can possibly imagine by encouraging child labour in the Middle East. Kiddos are still chained to their machines – Dickensian ain't in it. Supply and demand of course, but where you represent the demand . . . If you must buy a hand-made carpet, at least buy an old one so at least whoever was forced to make it is dead. There is no demand anywhere in the Middle East for modern hand-knotted carpets . . . except from you.

Not Haggling

Oh please, don't haggle over bus tickets or things like oranges or loaves of bread which have prices prominently displayed. (Needless to say except at tourist sites.) It is just embarrassing all round. Often the guy will reduce the price just to get you out of his shop, especially if you are a twenty-stone German in shorts who is beginning to shout.

Hand to Mouth

Living for most people in the Middle East is pretty much like this: food, family, money, food, family, money, day after day. Poverty is time-consuming in the extreme. One little addition to the family budget is enough to make society crack straight open. Take the subsidies off bread? You are looking at big riots at best, and if you are the president you are looking at exile, a new job or a long rope.

AID AND CORRUPTION

A lot of governments are in the position of having their main source of foreign revenue being Aid, either from within the region or from outside. The problem is a simple one: if you donate money you have to make it payable to someone – writing 'the people of Egypt' on a cheque is not exactly going to be cashable. It is terribly tempting when you are looking at a cheque for a few million dollars with your name on it just to say: 'My kids could use a new plane' and pocket the lot of it. The overseas bank accounts of a lot of the fat cats of the region could use a thorough examination.

Physical Aid runs into the same sort of problems albeit slightly lower down the ladder. US Aid 'not for sale' wheat and rice is for sale in every souk in the Middle East, and unless you believe this is an American plot to put local producers out of business (as many locals do) the most logical explanation is that some Mr Greedy in the equation has flogged it. Aid encourages corruption, and may even deliberately do so. Certainly it doesn't trouble the Aid organisations what the hell happens to the stuff they send. They do fine in the tax-free, good-salary leagues and even if they ship time-expired offal to be sold off by local criminals, they can still say, 'We sent 20,000 tons of wheat to Zongo.' What does it matter to them if the wheat is unfit for human consumption? (They don't have to eat it.) Or if the medicines are past their sell-by date – 'Much cheaper old fellow, fancy another office?' Still it's a racket like anything else and there are honourable exceptions, mostly the small medical charities. Very honourable exceptions, so good for them.

Bribery

This is a tricky one for the holidaymaker. In very general terms you can sometimes bribe yourself out of trouble, but if you don't know the socially correct way of doing this (i.e. the face-saving way of handing the cash over) things could end up worse. If you simply say to an official, 'Here is money. Let me go,' you will outrage him, triple your sentence/fine and generally get into a whole heap of additional trouble. What you have done is suggest to the man that you think he can be bribed, which may indeed be the case, but presenting this directly to him has called his honour into question. Generally avoid trying to bribe anyone directly. If, however, he hints a small financial contribution is called for, you can try it. On your own head be it.

REAL ENEMIES

The Middle East tends to be vulnerable to political unrest, which can sometimes be attributed to non-representative and at times downright capricious government, sometimes to outside meddling. Most Arab countries fall out on a regular basis, though they also make up and become friends again. The underlying structural problem tends to be between the Arab powers and the two regional but non-Arab powers, Turkey and Iran. At the moment there is a great deal of tension between Saudi Arabia and Iran; this could change, but it's been a constant for a while. Mostly this manifests itself in the small Gulf States. Iran is surreptitiously tinkering with the internal affairs of these little countries, while Saudi has defence agreements with most of them. Where this seems most likely to lead to trouble is Bahrain.

Bahrain has a vociferous, largely Shia opposition which is repressed by the Emir but backed by the Iranians. There have been bombs, protests and demands for some kind of democratic assembly. The lid still isn't firmly back on the troubles, things tend to flare up and then die down again. In essence this is a proxy war between Saudi and Iran: if the royals start going down in the Gulf States, Iran hopes this will push the Saudi monarchy the way of the Shah. Iran treasures the hope that Saudi will go belly-up after a popular revolt. Saudis and Americans *dread* this scenario and will do virtually anything to prevent it. This partly accounts for the current demonisation of Iran in the West. Hence Bahrain, and what happens to its ruling family is of interest to all the big players both inside and outside the region. Could America intervene, with a straight face, to replace the Emir of a tiny island? Who had been overthrown and replaced by a democratic assembly? Tricky, very tricky. The post-war weakening of Iraq has been of benefit to the Iranians – they now feel safer throwing their weight around in the Gulf, and the recent augmentation of the Iranian navy suggests that, at a pinch, they might consider invading a Gulf State. If the Iranians intervened in Bahrain to support a 'democratic' coup, the West would go frantic. Thought Kuwait was of 'vital strategic interest' to the West? Just wait til the Americans start presenting Bahrain as our little chum in dire danger. Bullshit detectors will be reading critical within twenty-four hours. This is one of a number of regional flashpoints, but the key point remains the enmities between the big players.

Turkey too is viewed with suspicion by its Arab neighbours. Turkey has good, or at least cordial, relations with Israel, and strong trading links with Iran as well as the extensive dam system on the Tigris and Euphrates. The Turks were also the power which colonised much of the Middle East. So Turkey throwing its weight around is one thing which makes Arabs cosy up to each other. For the moment Turkish foreign policy is focused on the central Asian republics where they have linguistic links, but if this changes and Turkey starts playing around in Middle Eastern politics there could be trouble. Recently a big gas deal between Turkey and Iran signalled that these two big powers were coming to some sort of accommodation (see 'visiting' below), which made the Arabs immediately nervous, and if Turkey and Iran show signs of sticking their noses into northern Iraq, a round of significant inter-Arab visiting will no doubt start off.

For Arab leaders, visiting is a big deal. If an Arab leader visits someone he hasn't seen for a while, it is often a prelude to a shift in allegiances. Jordan is particularly addicted to changing friends at the moment. Jordanian relations with Iraq have gone from being close allies to blaming Iraq for the recent Jordanian riots. (The fact that the government had doubled the prices overnight was not considered to be a more likely cause, for some reason.) So visiting is important, but so is staying home. Some Arab leaders don't much like to leave home. It is just so embarrassing if you are deposed while at a conference. If an Arab leader cuts down on the visiting, the odds are high that there is some kind of unrest in his country.

SURREAL ENEMIES

The other non-Arab power in the region is Israel. There is little point in rehashing all the arguments on both sides, but the Arabs see Israel as a dangerous and alien colonising power, backed by America and armed up to the teeth. Two Arab policies ran more or less in tandem until recently. The first was to ignore Israel and boycott her goods, the second was occasionally to attack her. Neither were particularly successful, so at the moment tentative moves to come to some kind of cold peace are being brokered by the Americans. It doesn't look too promising. Israel is reluctant to relinquish military gains and there are all these Palestinians who are going to have to live somewhere other than inside a greater Israel. It seems an insoluble enmity and still has potential to cause war, though the Arabs would be reluctant to try it until they thought they had achieved some kind of nuclear capacity. Israel is clearly absolutely dedicated to making sure this doesn't happen, but the real problems will come when either Saudi or

Iran develops nuclear capacity. Saudi in particular, being an ally of America, would be politically tricky to bomb. I'm sure the Israelis would think of something though.

The Shouting, the Shouting

Very popular is recreational shouting. It is often difficult to work out what is going on. It may just be a bit of light shopping, or the fall of the republic, but each in their own little way works better with shouting (preferably lots of it), coupled with waving things around – banners, bags of oranges, heads of infidels on pointed sticks, whatever is relevant. You can probably spot the difference between mass insurrection and a shopping spree.

Effing and Blinding

Sudanese Arabic contains an excellent insult: 'Son of a Woman who fucks on a Railway Platform'. Egyptian includes such memorable bits of social criticism as 'He would eat his profits from a dog's arsehole.' Arabic is poetic and that applies to its insults as well.

Giving of Gifts

In general terms you will end up spending much of your time with people who are poor, proud and being exceedingly generous to you. The longer you travel in the area the more you realise that the real trick is not avoiding being ripped off but rather the ability to present gifts to people in a suitable manner. If invited to an Arab household or wandering round a non-touristy area where hospitality might be offered, try and carry two or three little non-expensive bits and pieces which you can give to the kids of the family treating you to dinner – things like pocket-knives, postcards of your home town — anything little and foreign. You can do this with a clear conscience (always ask the father's permission first). If the infants seem particularly shy, give it to the father to give to them.

Baksheesh Mein Herr

Of course there are a few scumbaggies in any country who prey on tourists: very much a minority and never particularly dangerous, but wearing and time-consuming. The mildest form of this affliction is people who seek to attach themselves to you and perform unwanted services until you open your wallet. Taxi drivers are addicted to this sort of trouble-making. As a rule of thumb any taxi that is waiting outside your hotel is going to contain one irritating, expensive and persistent nuisance who'll overcharge you and take a fit if you try to get into any other taxi. Taxi drivers are horrible in any country but ones that prey on tourists in the Middle East are the chaff that the lord driveth away. Try and avoid taxis parked outside hotels, you are better off flagging one down in the street.

Madmen

Lots of them are loose in the Middle East. Arabs still have a community that cares on a personal rather than a state basis so families with mad relatives normally look after them. Non-dangerous nutters are often wandering around the streets muttering away and getting into confused arguments with themselves or you, unless they are ruling the countries, in which case they are whipped around in motorcades. You do get a certain number of flashers (from those on the streets rather than from the motorcades).

Moroccan Role

Morocco is feeling unloved these days. It's an odd sort of image problem. Morocco's distinguishing characteristic seems to be unpopularity. They are ignored and marginalised at meetings of the Arab League and their application to join the EU was given a real *nul points* raspberry. Other Arabs insist vehemently that Moroccans are not 'like' Arabs. No wonder Moroccans feel rejected. The whole world seems to be badmouthing them. Even my guide book was being distinctly evasive on the subject. Bursts of personalised venom about street hustlers were followed by guilty though airy generalisations about how nice some of them must be *really*.

You'll find out the problem from day one: 'You're never alone with a Moroccan.' It's mostly well intentioned and who minds crashing out a few cigarettes a day, but this constant incoming traffic wears you down eventually. The hustlers you can learn to chase off. They rattle a lot of tourists though. Tangier is particularly bad and is maybe not the best town to start with. There they *will* try to sell you a doe-eyed boy or a wardrobe-sized lump of adulterated hashish. Otherwise it's pretty innocuous stuff, the worst that happened to me was a guy hanging a snake round my neck and demanding money. You might end up simply paying him to go away. If it's that or inserting the snake into its owner in front of a crowd of 200

Moroccans, a small donation to Save the Snake is probably the safer bet.

Morocco is often the first poor country travellers hit and it's a shock to some systems. A guy tapping a cigarette off you is doing it not for the fun of it but because he wants a cigarette and hasn't the immediate money to undertake such a major investment. You meet these bleached-out airheads, or the Surf Nazis on tour, who moan their idiot faces off about being ripped off, but if you must rush off to a bazaar when you're stoned out of your head and start buying large lumps of lapis lazuli or Berber rugs, you will quite properly be robbed blind. Anything that involves paying money to sit on top of an animal is liable to be an expensive mistake as well. Just remember that the phrases 'to pester a foreigner' and 'to enjoy yourself' have identical meanings to a Moroccan, so take it easy, learn to enjoy being hassled or at least to see the funny side of it. It's one way of passing the time and what else were you planning on doing?

'Yikes it's Casablanca, it's the middle of the night and I'm being felt up by a sheep-faced Mauritanian prostitute.' Relax: it's only another bar. Right at the seediest end of bars in the Middle East are those in Morocco's biggest port. Beer by the Moroccan state monopoly, customers by Hieronymus Bosch. And they are – there are some seriously deranged fashion statements being made out here. The combination of Moroccan criminals, east European sailors and large African prostitutes make for unsightly viewing. As does the beer: Flag (are they trying to tell me something?) comes in bottles that are hideously small. Stork, another very odd name for a beer when you come to think of it, at least contains an acceptable amount. There is a bracing anti-foreign undercurrent, especially in the bars. Moroccans take offence easily, but any nonsense you get into in the way of arguments seems to cool down before you get into serious trouble. Moroccans are sick of the bad press they receive and it sometimes shows.

The towns are complex tangles of restaurants, tiny hole-in-the-wall shops and tourist bazaars. Moroccan private houses look drab, closed against the outside world. An invitation to visit should be jumped at though. Behind the wall you offer to the world there is a whole world of extended families, sunlight and peace. Life isn't easy for most Moroccans. You stare half-hypnotised out of the train window at stretches of wrecked and unproductive land, the occasional low, flat house, wondering how *can* Morocco sustain anywhere near its current population. Basically, it can't. Morocco's big towns are far too big, there aren't enough jobs, estimates of unemployment run as high as 50 per cent, which can't be right, or can it? People are sitting around waiting for something to do all over the country. So then how many Moroccans does it take to change a bus wheel? The answer is, 'More than forty.' That's all there were on the bus and after they had removed the wheel and started dismantling the entire rear axle, losing important-looking nuts and bolts, sawing away at what looked like the suspension, everyone got involved at least to the extent of offering advice. Community *kif* smoking just muddled the whole procedure. I sat through a few hours of this but when the least obviously stoned of the passengers emerged from under the bus and said, 'By God, we must have a mechanic,' I realised it was time to give up. The bus was clearly being taken to bits for the sheer pleasure of it. They are probably still there now.

There simply isn't much of anything for Moroccans to actually do. If you are unemployed living on fifteen pence a day, why not go and pester that tourist? He might be an easy way to get a free beer or a couple of cigarettes, that's how it more or less goes, hardly being malicious, just poor and at a loose end. Tourists get themselves into a terrible state about all this. They eventually divide into those who have become paranoid and those who will get paranoid if they do go for a smoke with that extravagantly villainous-looking dealer putting the bite on them. Travellers insist you'll get the shits before you are out of the airport yet, however hard I tried, it didn't happen. The food got cheaper, the locations more eccentric, but nothing. Just stop worrying about the place. Relax, you're in Morocco.

Got the shits yet?

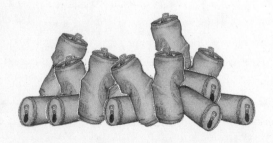

Power Rangers

KEEP SMILING

'No thanks' and a smile gets you past most hassling souvenir sellers – just put your hand to your heart to stress sincerity. You will probably lose your temper once or twice. Try not to feel too guilty, it does no harm to blow a gasket once in a while, and it means it's possible to do the smiling and 'no thanks' bit for a while again. Don't hit people or push them out of the way – it can cause an intractable shouting squabble which spreads out in all directions. If someone actually grabs you in an attempt to pull you into his shop, disengage yourself abruptly by all means, but don't just whop the guy. If someone is following you, bugging you and generally not going away, especially if you are a woman, you can bellow *'Ayyab'* (Shame) and normally this gets things sorted out, as more respectable Arab men chase off the chaser.

BUT DO THEY REALLY LOVE ME?

Of course not. You will generally be treated with great charm and politeness throughout the region, but why on earth should they? A certain percentage of the population will see you as a financial or sexual opportunity. Otherwise you are a time-wasting nuisance – you can't speak the language, you behave peculiarly by local standards, you might be mildly entertaining but that is largely because life is pretty dull.

It is still a lot better than the way Arabs are treated in Europe. You will not be banged-up by cops in sex criminal uniforms for having a moustache (France). Or punched senseless for having a suntan (France and everywhere else too). In fact it reflects great credit on the Arab world as a whole that you are treated so courteously throughout the region. It is foolish to expect to be 'liked' in addition to all the politeness. When you consider the amount of misery we have inflicted on the Arabs over the years, you are lucky not to be hanging from the nearest lamp-post.

MAPWORK

Take a look at your map of the Middle East. Notice anything more than averagely strange about these borders? Lots of straight lines maybe? Lots of borders which are simply marked as undefined? Quite a number of strangely-shaped countries? Odd disparity in sizes? Look at Jordan – see that huge notch in the eastern border, apparently known as Winston's Hiccup? While carving up this end of the Med, Churchill had apparently had too much to drink and bloop went the Jordanian border. Pretty depressing for Arabs to reflect that their lands were carved up by a load of drunks. If we felt guilty about this we could always invite a stoned-out-of-their-face Moroccan team to re-draw Europe's boundaries. Well, it might work. In a way Iraq does have a point about Kuwait. It was a province of Iraq (well kind of) until the British in a fit of late empire levity promoted it from mud fort to independent country. It must have been a hell of a lunch.

"IT MUST HAVE BEEN A HELL OF A LUNCH!"

Bad Landlords

What else did Britain do when we were running the show? Well, we played shuffle the kings with Jordan, Iraq and Saudi to no very coherent end. King Hussein managed to survive this nonsense. We tried to shore up a monarchy in Egypt and Iraq as well, but let's face it, when it came to propping up Middle Eastern monarchies Britain wasn't a great success. The other thing we left the Middle East was a whole new state staffed by crazy imperialists, just so they wouldn't forget us.

So Were the French any Better?

In short, no. Though they did go in for some wonderfully stupid ideas. If one thing can be said it is that they hung on to their colonies for too long. They even went as far as telling the

Algerians that they *were* French – understandably this went down like a cup of cold sick.

And What About the Americans?

Americans have an odd view of colonialism partly based on their geographical position, partly on their turn-of-the-century kudos gained from being a trading but non-colonial power in the Far East. Americans go in for proxy colonies. In essence this is more sensible than the British system of turning up in funny clothes and building railway stations which, at least initially, provided much mirth. The American system is leverage- and economics-based. Fine-tuned during the 1973/4 oil crises, it boils down to two policies (to be delivered respectively in Robert de Niro and Arnold Schwarzenegger voices):

A) Fuck with us and we'll starve you to death.

B) Fuck with us and we'll bomb you flat.

Egypt is a nice simple case of A. Iraq of B (and, post the UN sanctions, A). No wonder some Arabs get almost nostalgic for nineteenth-century colonialists. I'm not sure if sub-imperial gangsterism is what one expects from 'The World's Policeman'.

Ah Zose Russians

In comparison with any of the above, Soviet involvement in the Middle East has always seemed extraordinarily naive, and my, did they ever suffer for it. Arabs know a sucker as soon as they see him, and though Russian intentions post-war were honourable, and a genuine attempt to help was made with the Aswan Dam and various arms sales, the Arabs simply responded by taking advantage. I'm only guessing, but I imagine the percentage of

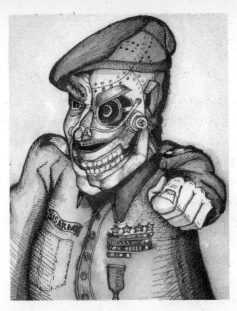

Russian arms in the Middle East which have actually been paid for is pretty much zero. The real reason for Russian disengagement from the Middle East was that by the mid-Eighties they were not only getting sick of being ripped off but, more seriously, kept being put into distinctly precarious political positions by their supposed allies. Both Russia and America were nearly brought into direct confrontation several times by their Middle Eastern allies. The Russians have given up. The Americans are so leg-trapped by the Jewish lobby at home that they are stuck with being an unwilling ally of Israel forever. This is why America spends so much time trying to broker the 'Peace Process' in the Middle East; it ain't altruism, that's for sure. The Americans hope that everyone will sign some piece of paper or another and they can get back to a more isolationist policy. Fat chance, but that's what they hope for.

THE GULF WAR

The aftermath of this hasn't really worked its way through yet but, when travelling in the Middle East, avoid discussing the Gulf War. To the Arabs this was as great a humiliation as the 1967 war with Israel, made worse by the fact that Arab armies and governments colluded in the destruction of a major Arab country by the West. Recriminations are still going on and the long-term outcome cannot be predicted, but it will probably speed up the change in governments in the region which is going to really boom boom shake the room in the late 1990s, and you can bet your bottom dollar pro-Western governments are going to be rare as hen's teeth by the year 2000.

As after the Six Day War, anger is combined with a feeling of impotence. As Arabs can't effectively retaliate against America, a lot of this resentment ends up being directed at their own leaders for their supine acceptance of the American agenda. The Arab world's response to this crisis was an ill co-ordinated mess and the leaders were still squabbling while the whole situation spiralled out of control. This has particularly increased the vulnerability of the Gulf States. As the Emirs were particularly craven in turning their backs on other Arab states and begging for American assistance, Bahrain and Qatar have alienated large parts of their own populations and undermined the legitimacy of all the Gulf monarchies. In the case of Bahrain, an additional worrying factor is Iranian meddling, which isn't helping on the stability front.

The biggest and least visible effect was probably on the Saudis. The fiction, diligently maintained, that Saudi, while an ally of America, was not what you might call actually *dependent* on them, was blown apart. Whole sections of the non-royal Saudi population resented this furiously, and still do. The Americans may have harmed their long-term Middle East policy on this one. If one of the Gulf Emirates or Qatar loses its royal family, that could drag the Saudi royal family down as well. Oooh, wouldn't the Americans just have a fit if that happened.

Iraq itself is being treated shamefully by the international community, and don't think the Arab world has forgotten about that. The policy seems to many to have been one of indiscriminate destruction followed by what is in effect starving the population to near-death. How long this policy of maintaining sanctions will remain in place remains to be seen, but if Saddam one way or another manages to sit it out, his prestige in the region may actually be increased, unlikely though that may seem from a Western point of view. That presumably is why the undeclared sub-text of the UN sanctions is: no lifting of the sanctions until all weapons of mass destruction (including Saddam Hussein) are removed. The Americans are praying someone assassinates the bugger sooner or later, but he has proved tenacious, though he can't exactly be Mr Popular down in the empty souks.

In Kuwait itself, God alone knows what the long-term effects will be. The Emir and the members of Al Sabah PLC didn't exactly endear themselves to the population at large by making a mass dash for Saudi, leaving the non-royal population to sit out a horrible occupation, where torture was routine and nearly every family lost relatives, often in the most sickening circumstances. The Emir has made some vague promises about introducing democracy of some limited kind, but so far no dice. Probably Kuwait is as vulnerable to internal instability as any of the small Gulf states.

This has little practical effect on your travels except to the extent that some royal families in the Gulf region are going to go down like a pack of cards in the foreseeable future and you should plan on not being in town when it happens. If you are in a country when it goes belly-up, either get out pronto or if that isn't feasible stay away from major towns where most of the real trouble will be going on. Nice time to chill out in a beach resort? Not a bad idea. If the army seem to be getting involved stay away from airports which tend to be much squabbled over and plan on leaving overland.

'THE DIARY OF AN UNKNOWN SOLDIER'

I live with my comrades in arms three metres underground. We are armed with rifles and machine guns. These weapons have been useless against our enemies who fight only from the safety of their jet planes. Still sometimes one of our detachment fires away at some distant flying machine. Me, I go into our bunker at the first sound of approaching aircraft. The bunker would be useless if it took a direct hit, but it has saved me once already when they dropped anti-personnel bombs on us. Many little bombs come down and explode. Three men from my squad died. They have not been replaced. The big bombs though are aimed at our artillery. Most of them miss, but they've dropped so many that there is no functioning artillery that I know of.

My squad is not considered reliable. It is true we are not reliable. That is why we do not operate the artillery. That is why we are not the crew of a tank. That is why they have not given us anti-tank weapons. I am no professional soldier but I am not stupid. If the Americans come they will come in tanks and our rifles will be as useless as they are against the flying bombers. I suppose I would be no safer in Basra. The Americans have been bombing residential areas. Why not, they seem to have plenty of bombs. There is certainly one left for our bunker, it has simply not arrived yet.

Many people have deserted, that is what I have heard. If we talked about deserting our sergeant would send us away to be executed. He is not a bad man, I like him. I suppose if I were the sergeant and heard my men talking about deserting I would have to send them away to be executed too. Who cares? Give Kuwait back to the Americans and Kuwaitis. Not that they deserve it. But mostly I think about food and I wait, just like the others. Several times we have been cut off from fresh water, we filtered muddy water through a coffee filter. When you are thirsty enough you will drink anything. They say driving a water truck is one of the most dangerous jobs in this war. Driving any truck is dangerous. It is good, the weather is cool, we need less water. We were talking quietly, Yasar Abdul, Jarah Kish and myself, when the planes approached. We squatted down, but we could tell they were high overhead, and they passed without striking at us and I thought, how can I be happy when they are going to murder my friends, wives and children? But we did not talk about the war. Yasar, who was a clerk in a clothing store, tells how he hopes to be promoted soon to assistant manager. He does not really like the manager, but he tells little stories of sucking up to him. Kish says he should just start his own business. Kish has a stall from which he sells watches, and does very well. He wonders if his family is okay, but Jarah, who is a street-sweeper and uneducated, tells funny stories. He does not know they are street versions of traditional stories from the great literature of our country.

Tonight the deadline came and there was no attack. I think they would have attacked at midnight if they were going to attack. I was on guard duty and I was afraid. I heard from another guard that all of the Americans were near Kuwait, that we are safe here, the fighting will all be to the east.

*   *   *

They did not take my diary or my pencil yet. Everyone is asleep, but I fear sleep and write by the moonlight. The other guard was wrong. We had only a few minutes' warning. The planes and helicopters came in, and someone must have been awake when they passed because we heard there were tanks coming and the sergeant ordered us up into the trench. The tanks came fast and we fired at them. What else was there to do? We could not outrun them. Along the line men waved white flags, but the tanks fired at us anyway. There were armoured personnel carriers too with bulldozers behind them.

To my left a shell went off. I felt the blast against my clothing, a shock of sand mixed with blood and flesh. The Sergeant, Yasar Nebat and Abdul were gone. I took a white rag, an old t-shirt, and waved it overhead. Only my arm was above the line of the sand. My comrades lay low to the right. Along the line men stood up, fired, lay back down. Their tanks no longer fired so many rounds of artillery, they had changed to machine-gun fire, coming quickly closer. When a bullet hit my white flag, I sank down in the trench. In front of our trench was a larger trench designed to stop tanks. There was no gunfire from along our line near us, and Jarah managed to make a white rag from his clothing which he waved over his head. We heard much rumbling, engine noises. I didn't know what it was then, but it must have been the bulldozers filling the tank trench. The noise grew louder. I forced myself to look up. A great wall of sand was approaching. I screamed and ran along our trench. The wave of sand crested behind me, onto Jarah Kish, and the others. Soldiers with guns stood on the bulldozers, behind the great blades.

If I had had a gun I would have fired at them, but I had thrown it away. An American soldier appeared before me, the muzzle of his gun practically in my stomach. He motioned downwards and I fell to my knees. To either side of me tanks streamed over the new roads the bulldozers had made, over the bodies of my friends and comrades. I do not like war, but I can never forgive the Americans, they are cowards who hide behind their machines. I should not write this, the guards will find it and who knows what they will do to me.

> From 'The Diary of an Unknown Soldier: Gulf War'
> Reprinted with the permission of *The Stake* magazine.

Islam

Islam is most usually translated as 'submission' which is what it is – you submit to the word of God as made manifest in the Koran. No weak-assed Anglican crap here. The Koran is the word of God and you submit to that, full stop. You pray five times a day, you give alms, you believe. It's strange to us. Our lack of faith is a bit puzzling to the Moslems. Faith underpins every Moslem's life; even disreputable boozers and womanisers are still secure in the comfort and peace of mind that Islam confers. Lucky them. It also means Moslems are more at ease with Europeans with a solid faith and no need to gab on about it, or question it.

Speaking as an atheist, I can recommend Islam well in advance of any of the other monotheistic religions. It is more modern – no don't laugh – than Christianity or Judaism and contains better prose, poetry and punishments than either of the others. It is a respectable religion, and one to respect for the duration of your stay. So the call to prayer wakes you up at four in the morning? At least Moslems don't turn up at your door whenever you get round to cooking, in dark suits, wanting to chat about 'witnessing' or some such tosh. No Moslem will seek to convert you, play an acoustic guitar badly, or organise a prayer jive in the name of progress. Like I say, a respectable religion. Never, however cheeky you are feeling, insult Islam, the name of God, or make a joke at the expense of Islam or the prophet Mohammed. Anyone should be able to respect that.

THE CALL TO PRAYER

Mostly because of the sheer lack of imagination of television and radio journalists, the call to prayer is habitually used as a sort of theme tune for programmes dealing with the Middle East. It is distinctive and the fact that the first call is very early in the morning means it sticks in many travellers' minds. It can actually be extraordinarily beautiful coupled with the sun setting over a city, or out in the middle of nowhere.

Five times a day the faithful are called to prayer, and the Moslem orientates himself to Mecca whether he is in the street, at home or in the mosque. He then prostrates himself several times in a prescribed manner, reciting the *fathia* (the opening verse), and at times other *surah* (verses) of the Koran.

CONVERSION

A lot of people do convert to Islam. In America the Nation of Islam is primarily a black movement; white converts are rarer – having a more individualistic and frankly racist perception of Islam, they tend to perceive Islam as a threat rather than a valid option. Bit of a mistake, but the Americans get all hot under the collar and have stopped looking for reds under their beds and are now peeking around for Moslems.

RAMADAN

What a mistake; you're in the Middle East during Ramadan. A month of public fasting from dawn to dusk. This includes you –

eating in public during Ramadan is frowned on no matter where you're from. While it is not actually forbidden, nothing is open this side of posh hotels and the odd restaurant – even smoking in the street is a no-no. Everything is closed, everyone is bad-tempered and half-starving. The dewy-eyed Arabist will say things liven up at night. Indeed they do, but if your idea of fun is eating pumpkin seeds at three in the morning you should be ashamed of yourself. Fancy a drink? Well, Cyprus is about your nearest bar. You can actually drink during Ramadan but only in Hilton/Sheraton type places at budget-biting prices. Turkish and Egyptian resorts are sometimes possible but you have to have every bottle wrapped up in pink toilet paper so that you don't provoke local insurrection when drinking in public. If you know sympathetic expatriates you might get a few crumbs from their booze orders, but drinking a time-expired bottle of crème de menthe locked in a hotel bedroom listening to an eighteen-hour screamed and amplified sermon is about as gloomy a social experience as can be imagined.

RELIGION: NONE

This is mostly aimed at dyed-in-the-wool atheists who when filling in their landing cards put: 'Religion: None'. Really, don't bother, the subsequent earache can hold you up at any given airport for hours. The idea of someone without religion is anathema to Arabs. You will be asked continually about your religion in the Middle East – unless you know the person particularly well, don't say atheist. The subsequent conversation is one of the most boring this side of building cathedrals out of matchsticks. It more or less boils down to the guy picking up every item within reach and saying, 'And who made this then?' This can drag on for hours and it is impossible to stop him, short of aggravated assault.

FOOTNOTE FOR CHRISTIANS

Moslems have a lot of respect for Christianity, indeed Jesus (*Isa*) is considered to be one of the prophet Mohammed's forebears and is in the Koran, as is John the Baptist (*Yahia*). The principal objection to Christianity, and quite a valid one if you know your early church history, is the attribution of divine characteristics to a mortal. This is considered to be blasphemous to the highest degree.

FRIDAY

Friday is the Moslem sabbath and pretty gloomy it is too. This is the only time you might feel Islam to be sinister and threatening. The two-hour amplified sermons sound alarming even after years in the region – just a sort of howl of outrage while the streets fill up with people kneeling and praying. It always seems a bit creepy. The 'Keep Friday Frightening' campaign is not needed. Arabic sermons sound well, hm err, unique? And when there are 3,000 echoing round town, maybe time to stay in and write a few postcards? It is all more or less over by lunchtime.

MOSQUE VISITING

Take a kind of conservative line on this one. That is, don't visit mosques at all, except ones obviously geared to deal with tourists. Islam is an intensely respectable religion and you will be a lot more respected if you stay out of their places of worship. The fact is, even if you are not unwelcome you are unexpected, and however much you cover up, or take your shoes off, you will end up causing some bother. Unfortunately most readers will disregard this and visit mosques. So at the very least, dress respectably, don't take photos (especially of people at their devotions), don't wear shoes inside any mosque, and leave immediately and without any fuss if you are asked to. Keep quiet as well, this is a living religion.

Some of the more conservative countries don't let foreigners in any mosques and none like it. Turkey is the most relaxed about foreigners visiting mosques, but avoid going in when they are full of people praying, as this is considered bad-mannered at best. In mosques that are relatively used to tourists, like the Blue Mosque in Istanbul, your problem will be touts who demand money for showing you round. There is no entry fee for the mosque whatever anyone tells you and there is certainly not an additional payment required because you've seen people praying. Other countries are not so keen on visitors. Saudi and most of the Gulf countries don't allow foreigners in mosques. Egypt, apart from two or three mosques in Cairo and one in Luxor, doesn't really approve. And just in case you are too bone-headed to guess it, don't go anywhere near a mosque smelling of booze. Stay away from mosques unless they are meant to be really spectacular, and if you do go, try and arrange your visit in the company of a local acquaintance, to ensure you don't cause offence or insult.

MECCA

Turn to God. One of the obligations of Islam is to make (if financially possible) the pilgrimage to Mecca. The numbers involved in the annual *Hajj* are simply incredible. Millions of Moslems make the trip every year. The Saudis, while proud of their role as the custodians of the two holy places (Mecca and Medina), have realised that it is a logistic nightmare and increasingly a political one. Protests are staged, people get crushed, tunnels collapse, panic breaks out among the packed crowds. Security is the biggest headache for the Saudis. The none too paranoid fear is that someone will call for the overthrow of the Saudi monarchy from Mecca during the *Hajj*. Iranian pilgrims are viewed with particular suspicion, but trouble can come from any group at short notice.

Non-Moslems are not allowed into Mecca or Medina: if you get too close, signposts warn you that you are entering a religious no-go zone. Don't even think about disobeying them. Even discounting the sheer dullness of infiltrating a religious scrum of over two million international fanatics, the penalties are liable to be frightful. More seriously, European converts to Islam can run into trouble getting visas to go on the *Hajj*. If you are a white convert to Islam it would be sensible to get a supporting letter from your local mosque before applying for a visa and even then you will have to put up with a lot of suspicion during your pilgrimage.

The Citadel

In modern Israeli iconography, as befits a country which has produced far more history than can be consumed locally, the protracted siege and the heroic defence of the citadel of Massada, although it happened 2,000 years ago, loses nothing in the telling. For the disinterested traveller unsure of how this could possibly affect his happy holiday in sunny Israel, fear not. They liked it so much, you are flying into the remake.

An eerie obsession with ancient hard times manifests itself from the moment you touch down at Ben Gurion Airport – it's straight into modern-day Fortress Israel. Siege mentality assumes a personal relevance as you answer up to a hundred questions from nutbag security guards at the airport. Search procedures can be pretty rigorous. If you are a single non-Jewish male you may be asked the same set of questions several times, so it could be worth preparing a hand-out. This, by the way, is not the time or place to get facetious, or to mention that you plan putting on a tea towel and running off to play with the Palestinians. Just remember, it's nothing personal, Israelis are paranoid about everyone. Language in Israel is a minefield – confusing your *salaams* and *shaloms* is a recipe for disaster. Names of places aren't much safer: say 'the Wailing Wall' to a Palestinian or 'Al Haram Sharif' to an Israeli and expect a prolonged bout of the sulks. Maps are quite as schizophrenic; very old maps tend to get confiscated on arrival, as they show Palestine to actually be a country and the Israelis prefer to confiscate these to save you from confusion. Safest is to pretend an absolute geographic and historical ignorance as, surprise surprise, these are touchy subjects. Everything is.

For the Jews of the world, flying into Tel Aviv is the start of a joyous pilgrimage to their promised land, but like the American generals who were airlifted in and out of Saigon during the final stages of the Vietnam War, their reports that all is fine and dandy have to be discounted. Israelis are much more acutely aware of how precarious the real situation is. They *know* they are under siege, a siege moreover which requires constant vigilance, training and world-wide pan-handling even to maintain a defensive status quo. If you put a whole nation on guard duty for fifty years a certain amount of battle fatigue and callousness floats to the surface. Israelis are mutating under the strain. After a few beers, Jewish visitors begin to loosen up and admit that while they love being in the holy land, Israelis themselves can be arrogant and incredibly unfriendly. Personally I'd add terrifying to that list – Israeli eye contact translates into 'I can kill you any time I want, but not today, so lucky you.' All these hyena-eyed soldiers made me extremely jumpy.

Israel makes a lot of people almost deliriously happy, but it makes a great number of people inside its territories desperately miserable. The Palestinian population is in the position of a householder who has been successively forced to give up the best rooms in his house, then all the rest of them, until today he is permitted only to live in the garden shed on condition he reports weekly for a damn stiff biffing from the new landlord.

So how on earth did two people who so obviously can't stand

the sight of each other end up living in the same piece of real estate? Step forward perfidious Albion. Britain pioneered this lets-put-two-wildcats-in-a-sack-see-how-they-get-on school of diplomacy.

Tel Aviv could be any new town built in the middle of nowhere for no particular reason other than surplus concrete. It does however have its moments. It is the only town in the world where you catch yourself leering at military patrols – some of the khaki starlets of the Israeli army are extremely eye-catching. Food is peculiar. Try a kosher Mexican pizza for which the word bastard could have been invented. Like everyone else, you soon take the road to Jerusalem – Tel Aviv seems stranger the further you get from it. What is this town doing in an Arab country? Did it get lost on its way home from the pub? Stumble into the wrong country and fall asleep?

Jerusalem represents without a doubt the most gruesome theological joke on earth. It's sacred to so many religions that only the discovery of Buddha's tomb is awaited to complete the set. The old city does look magnificent, a twisting mediaeval maze with beautiful architectural vignettes on every other corner, it's just overloaded with religious sites, each a tiny potential flashpoint. Peaceful it isn't. Jerusalem is pervaded by an unsurpassed atmosphere of malice, bigotry and hatred, as close to a tangible air of evil as anyone could wish to experience. Every local exudes a simmering rage. Crowds of tourists float by oblivious, lost in their religious dreams. This is all the more ironic as the locals are consumed by a wholly secular bitterness. If you had used Satan as a design consultant for a historical Disneyland you would probably have ended up with something so close to the old city of Jerusalem as to have rendered your journey unnecessary. Which would have been nice. Jesus may have ridden into Jerusalem on an ass, but it's been ass kicking since.

Whoever is top dog in the region wants Jerusalem – for the holy sites of course, but also seemingly for the pleasures of persecuting the other interested religions. These days it's the Israelis in control. Jerusalem is garrisoned by jumpy and downright violent-looking soldiers. It feels like an occupied city. If the Palestinians were back in control they'd probably be behaving much the same. Palestinians have been around for as long as anyone in the region, but they are going to have to get their act together pretty sharpish if they don't want to go the way of such original occupants of real estate as Aborigines or Red Indians. Something more substantive than the Norway accords is urgently needed. Better land for peace than war for land. Like it or not Palestine has been successfully invaded and occupied, not for the first time in its history, by an outside power – using as is traditional both fair means and foul to establish first a toe-hold and then a stranglehold. Compromise would seem to be the only answer but it isn't easy for either side, the hatreds run too deep. One could see the last Israeli and the last Palestinian fighting it out on the heap of rubble that was their country.

Both sides, when the opportunity presented itself, have behaved abominably. It seems to be an unbreakable cycle of murder and revenge. One solution might be to deport all the Palestinians to New Zealand and all the Israelis to Iceland – if nothing else it is the quickest way I can think of to produce an ICBM with a range of 10,000 miles. If you are thinking of a peaceful holiday, try somewhere less raddled by sectarian hatred: like Belfast.

Police and Thieves

CHECK POINTS

Standard throughout the region. National service means there are millions of poor souls in ill-fitting uniforms surplus to requirements. So they get stuck at check-points. Stopping you is probably the highlight of their day, so don't spoil it for them. If they want to tap a couple of fags off you, hand them out. If they want to search your bags or do a bit of mild swaggering, let them get on with it. Normally they will leave you alone as they have no particular instructions on 'how to deal with foreigners' and if in doubt will just ignore you. In countries where you need travel permits, photocopy the original and make as many copies as you might need. Being stuck at a check-point between 'Ugh' and 'Gibber' is almost inconceivably boring and something to play with is treated with great interest. If you hand over original documents or your passport you may be stuck for hours while they puzzle over your visa stamps, point and laugh at your passport photo, then try and memorise the whole thing. Handing over a photocopy keeps everyone happy. Your fellow travellers will not thank you if you enforce three-hour stops at every check-point. The soldiers will normally wave you through, if they have a copy of the relevant documents.

IN TOWN

Same kind of thing, there are flocks of bored soldiers all over the place. They may appear to be patrolling with the guns and that, but they are normally just wandering about and very rarely get given bullets. Patrols get gloomy and attach themselves to you to relieve the monotony of guarding whatever it was. In general these soldiers are not something to be fearful of. A group of twenty bored squaddies drove me out to Sana'a airport, not only abandoning their post but shooting a few dogs on the way out to keep me entertained – well worth the cigarettes.

BUT THEN AGAIN

Unusual uniforms mean soldiers who actually do things more military than scrounge cigarettes, and are to be avoided. Camouflage outfits that look like pizza toppings are a bad sign, mostly because the poor guys who have to appear in public in these clownish uniforms are bound to get a bit ratty. All black uniforms and ones that actually fit are other warning signs that these may be soldiers who get guns with bullets in them. Take it easy with soldiers, their interest in you is generally friendly, not malicious. However don't do the local equivalent of 'accompanying me to the station'. Once you are banged up, torture is routine and incompetent, though often fatal; once you are in prison the assumption is often that you are guilty and getting this sorted out is simply a matter of upping the voltage or hauling out another couple of teeth. In other words, 'Guilty until proven dead'.

CRUEL AND UNUSUAL PUNISHMENTS

Yemen is the place, if you like this kind of thing. There is a serious point to this section though. If you find yourself in the vicinity of a public execution, get out of the way as quickly as is possible. Otherwise you are likely to be pushed right up to the front row so you don't miss a drop. This can easily be fatal, as killing mobile targets with semi-automatic rifles (the practice in more civilised executions) places the front row in a certain amount of jeopardy. A front-row seat at a hacker slasher event (chopping off arms, legs, heads, etc.) will probably ruin your sleep for years (not to mention that nice white shirt you just put on). More pertinently, crowds get really pumped up at these events and it is possible they might turn on you afterwards as a dessert. You are simply too conspicuous ever to be really safe in any fired-up Arab crowd.

Crowds and power is the bottom line here. Middle Eastern mobs build up very quickly into all-round trouble. Partly because it is the only real method of protest available but also because it is just such fun torching rich people's houses and unpopular embassies. Any street argument which seems to be sucking in people who themselves get involved in the shouting rather than calming things down is one to stroll away from. A rare problem, but one to avoid.

PUBLIC SAFETY

This is a big plus, and one that you don't notice at first, because rather than something tangible, it is an absence of fear sensation.

Try this: late at night in your home town you are walking along a road on your own, and a group of young men is approaching from the opposite direction. Feel any fear? Translate the same scenario to the Middle East and bingo, no fear. As often as not, even in the biggest towns, you stop for a chat or at least exchange greetings. In general the area is safe, very safe. Just as reassuring is that if you shout for help, everyone within earshot comes racing up to see what is going on, and gathers round the guy who has given you trouble, ticking him off in no uncertain terms. You can sometimes get trouble in big cities late at night. Groups of young Arab men these days occasionally hassle or mug foreigners, so crime is not unheard of, just much rarer than in Europe. If you are on the receiving end of aggressive bother, either head for a crowded, well-lit street where you'll be safe, or buttonhole the first Arab you see and indicate the troublemakers and the odds are he'll see them off for you. Slums and shanty towns should be stayed out of after dark, as much because they have no lights and no coherent streets as because people are hostile. Anyway let's face it, you are hardly going to be wandering around some inchoate Cairo slum at three in the morning unless you are wrong in the head in the first place.

Women should be careful late at night in big cities, as with anywhere in the world – there are guys around who will sexually harass you, follow you and generally make you feel uneasy. Again, head for bright lights and crowds, or ask someone respectable to drive off the nasty boys. Most Arabs are gentlemen and it would be by no means unusual for whoever has helped you to see you back to your hotel.

CRIME

The likeliest person to steal from you in the Middle East is a backpacker. That shifty-eyed Austrian, who has just bored you witless on how he has 'saved' a nanopfennig by bullying some impoverished local, is a prime suspect. Theft does exist obviously, but is rare. It's unwise to relax completely, especially in Egyptian or Israeli beach resorts and touristy areas; but in general, honesty, even embarrassing honesty, is the rule. Violent crime is practically unheard of: even if you do get mugged, and it does happen occasionally, it is done with the utmost courtesy, with lots of soulful eye contact and apologies. Which is alarmingly pleasant.

Tourist Traps

There are people from your own country who you would cross the street to avoid back home, but find yourself lumbered with for the duration of your holiday. I found typical sub-groups of this genre are young, vaguely unattractive female students who have had so much sexual hassle from Arabs that they sign up like a particularly disagreeable flock of sheep to follow your itinerary. It can end up like travelling with puppies and the locals thinking that you are an unsuccessful pimp on holiday. Another common example is the fool who has got himself trapped in an incomprehensible transaction with a local crook and hopes you will be the person to sort out the increasingly acrimonious dispute. In this sort of case, try pretending to be another nationality. Safest thing in such situations may be to say, '*Yeshtye Dve Pivo*??' with a quizzical look (it means, 'Another two beers?' in Czech). There are almost no Czechs on holiday, so if he understands you, at least he'll have to buy you a beer before he involves you in whatever tedious problems he has.

ANOTHER TYPE OF TRAVEL BORE: THE MAN WHO KNOWS

The Middle East is littered with these people. I fall into this category. The little scumbag with the wire-rimmed spectacles who is earwigging your conversation, pretending he isn't, and looking supercilious at the same time. He is probably writing things in a notebook as well, looking deadly serious. Believe me these folk (me included) are writing shopping lists, have been living in the Middle East for ages and are bored out of their minds, yet they 'know' things. They may be able to be fluently obsequious in bad Arabic, they may know the best barber locally but they are as dull as a pie gets – well-intentioned sure, but that isn't much to say about anyone. Up to you, a local resident who speaks a bit of the language can come in handy occasionally, always full of tips which range from the worthless to the valuable – just work out how much of your holiday time it is worth wasting on these rather sad little cats.

OTHER EUROS

If you are getting worn down and lonely and just want to spend time with folk of your own nationality, head for the cafés recommended in your sensible guide book, hang out there, and choose carefully. If you think the man in the previous section is as bad as it gets, just wait til you've spent three hours with an Austrian scuba diver who describes each dive he has ever taken in real time. One hour at the bottom of the sea = one-hour anecdote. Aiie.

NON COMM

Assuming you don't speak much, or any, Arabic, you will end up once in a while stuck with someone who seems desperate to communicate, but with whom you don't have a language under the sun in common. These 'conversations' are common on buses and are simply mangled strings of noises, lots of smiles and a friendly Arab giving you sweets, cigarettes, nuts or whatever. Lots of eye contact, gestures which may mean something to either of you, but more probably don't, repeated production of his identity card for you to examine to prove that he is a *bona fide* Arab, not a Canadian travelling in disguise. Which is one more reason to learn a bit of Arabic as ten-hour conversations with a shared vocabulary of three words are, eventually, a bit of a pain in the neck.

The other side of the equation is *not* to assume that you will not be understood if you and your partner start grumbling on about, 'What a squalid bunch of losers there are on this bus,' or 'Oooh look at that poor ugly sod with the goitre.' Someone may well speak excellent English, and quite properly tell you not to be so rude about your fellow passengers, or his goitre. Speaking English is not always as private as you assume. A very common and absurdly Eurocentric attitude is that if an Arab speaks English, he will automatically want to come and speak with you. Why should he? He is out for a peaceful drink with friends and speaks first-class English, but maybe he reckons adding some dummy tourist to the company is none too brilliant an idea. If you get stuck, he will, out of courtesy, use his English to sort out whatever problem you have landed yourself in, but do not always assume this means the man is just dying to talk to you afterwards. A hell of a lot of Europeans do, but why? You might be a complete irrelevance to him, maybe he doesn't give a toss about your half-baked opinions on his country. Maybe he prefers the company of his own friends, his own gossip and concerns to listening to you yakking on about camel rides or Bedouin pottery. Strange isn't it? If you are specifically invited, sit down by all means, but don't impose yourself on people, just because your master race sensibilities mean you are convinced any Arab is prepared to drop his own business for the pleasure of talking to a complete stranger.

GETTING RID OF 'MY FRIEND' POLITELY

At some time in your trip you will find yourself saddled with a perfectly decent guy, someone who is quite pleasant for a couple of hours of chat, then begins to wear a bit thin, then gets boring, and then you start to think about throttling him. Now this fellow has been kind and helpful, he has bought you cups of tea, he is probably some kind of student and is just being friendly. It is obviously absurdly impolite to tell him to piss off when you've had enough of his company. He is probably just as bored as you are, but Arabs, out of a sort of endemic politeness, will suggest all sorts of things to do. The problem is like the Chinese finger trap – the more of these suggestions you accept, the more difficult it becomes to extricate yourself politely. This is often the stage when a visit to family or friends is suggested. You may well go along thinking that it may be dull as hell, but surely won't go on for too long. Don't do it! You're wrong.

You'll be lumbered sitting around drinking tea and eating nuts forever, in company you might well find uncongenial. If you are already getting slightly bored of your 'friend', make any (polite) excuse rather than go and visit his family. It becomes almost impossible to leave as various friends and relatives are produced. Arabs can spend longer doing nothing at all than seems conceivable and doing it with such patent kindness and gentleness that however bored you get, you are stuck there. After four hours of being introduced to everyone sentient in the neighbourhood and having bits of furniture or particularly exciting specimens of livestock introduced to you, you will be grinding your teeth.

And this is before the ordeal by photographs. Your 'friend' has three and a half million photographs of everyone he has ever met – 'This is me in military uniform', 'This is friend', 'This is another friend', 'This is wedding'. This sounds hellish enough, but just wait til you get the loonie who has foreign 'friends'. Another riffle of albums and there they are – 'This is Austrian friend' (gritting his teeth). 'This is Brazilian friend' (mopish-looking and who can blame him). 'This is Swedish girlfriend' (fat woman, obviously a complete stranger shaking her fist at the camera). And yes, you've guessed who is going to be next – you too will be there adding to the torture of some future guest. 'This is me with Scottish friend punching me on the nose.' Awful stuff really. The point here is not to put you off visiting Arabs, but to put you off visiting boring Arabs. If someone is 'borderline tolerance' over a couple of cups of tea in the local café, the odds are high that he isn't suddenly going to become wildly interesting over eight hours and 3,000 snapshots at home. If you suspect this is what your visit is going to be like, disengage yourself politely from him in public. Think of some formula by which you can dodge the house visit. Better a lie at this stage in the proceedings than both of you suffering agonies of boredom later.

Return

This seems to be a key term somehow, as much of the underlying melancholy of the Middle East is related to displacement. Cities are full of people who have been forced to leave their own villages. Tourist resorts are staffed by young men hundreds of miles from home earning next to nothing. Rich Gulf countries are run by lonely expatriate Egyptians and Jordanians. Palestinians don't even have a country left they could return to. Political exiles and students lead dull and frightening lives in Europe, either being patronised by well-intentioned students or being threatened with violence or deportation.

To return is not just a physical thing, it is also what one might term a spiritual problem. To return to what? An era where all the horrible things that happen don't happen? A time before Israel, before Turkey, before European involvement? When was that then? The retrospective golden age is very far away for Arabs. It's been a hard old road downhill since the great days of the Arab Empire, when Arabs had control over their own destinies. Like the Jews, in many ways the key is displacement and the hope of return. The Israelis may have achieved their dream of return but it was at the expense of others, who inherited the melancholy of wandering homelessness that the Jews sought to save themselves from. This displacement manifests itself in many intangible ways. In anger, in sorrow, in care for what they have left, whether it be children they dote on, keys to a family house bulldozed under a smart modern kibbutz block, titles to land that can never be redeemed. These scraps of half-effaced lives are very dear to those who have lost them.

It is possible to feel like an exile in your own country, even if you haven't been physically forced into a refugee camp. So leaving aside the Palestinians (as everyone tends to), think of the family living in some shanty town in the suburbs of Casablanca – they have no tenure, no right to stay there, no wish to stay there, but there they are. No way back to their village. Nothing for them to do if they could go home. Or that chain-smoking Jordanian customs official who is lousing up your day at a Saudi airport. Think he feels at home? Do you imagine he lives anywhere other than some squalid shitbox shunned by his Saudi employers? If it wasn't for the money, he wouldn't be there; he's counting the days til he can return. Obstructing you is just one way of making the time pass. You catch a glimpse of it sometimes when you see a plane-load of Yemenis going home after a couple of years of being treated like dirt in Saudi – the feeling of elation would move the plane without engines and that's just the temporary exiles.

It is not uncommon to see displaced Arabs crying after seeing their old village on the television. They know it is forever out of reach, captured by a foreign power, or bulldozed or collapsed. Some places simply have ceased to exist – the Nubians in Egypt had their villages drowned under the Aswan Dam – the only way back for them is to develop gills.

Villages can't support their populations – there is nothing for many to do except migrate to the swollen slums of the city. Cairo contains fourteen million people, most of whom would rather be back home on the family land. There isn't that much left to hang on to in the big cities. Islam provides a solace and clustering together with other exiles from the same part of the country provides some cohesion, but it is very much second-best.

When we travel there is always the basic premise that however long we are away there will be something more or less recognisable to return to. This isn't always the case for Arabs. Algerians who went to Europe to study now have a country they are too scared to return to waiting for them – so, expelled from Britain, they move on to a further exile working in Saudi or the Gulf States. No prospect of seeing family or friends. Palestinians have it even worse: they are welcome nowhere, and wherever they settle in the Middle East they remain resented outsiders who can never go home. Of course they are vulnerable to their host government's whims: Palestinians are forbidden to practise their professions in many of these countries, passports are never easy to come by and in times of trouble the nationals of the country they live in can turn against them. The vulnerability of the exile became all too clear after the Gulf War. The Palestinian population of Kuwait was over 100,000 before the Gulf War. Today it is barely a quarter of that. Where did they go? Where could they go? The Kuwaitis expelled those who they accused of 'collaboration', but it was by no means as simple as that – many were kicked out just for being Palestinian.

Recommended Reading

GENERAL

Peter Mansfield (1980) *The Arabs* London: Penguin
This is one of the best general introductions. Well-written and readable, though with some idiotic chapter titles – 'Sudan the loose-limbed giant' and 'Oman: the hermit disclosed' are two of the strangest, but despite these sort of misleading one-liners the book is fine.

Peter Slugett and Marion Farouk-Slugett (1993) *The Times Guide to the Middle East* London: Times Books
This is a good political overview, essay-length pieces on the countries of the region.

ISLAM

Alfred Guillaume (1977) *Islam* London: Penguin
A good introduction to the subject. If you are planning on doing business or living in the Middle East you are as well to have at least a sketch knowledge of Islam.

The Koran (1996) London: Garnet
This is a new translation just out which should be first-rate.

HISTORY

P. K. Hitti (1970) *A History of the Arabs* London: Macmillan
This is the standard text on Arab history. If you are interested in the history of the region this is the place to start. It has a problem common to all Arab histories — a great number of unfamiliar names in quick succession, but that can't be helped.

POLITICS AND PERCEPTIONS OF THE MIDDLE EAST IN THE TWENTIETH CENTURY

There are two key writers in this area: Edward Said and Noam Chomsky. Both are contentious figures.
Edward Said (1985) *Orientalism* London: Penguin
(1981) *Covering Islam* London: Penguin
(1987) *Blaming the Victims* London: Verso

Orientalism is an excessively difficult read, but worthwhile. Read it with a damp, ice-soaked towel on the side; it's tricky and the occasional lie-down with the towel over the forehead is needed except for real brain-boxes.
Covering Islam, on how the Western media (misre)present the Arabs and Islam, and *Blaming the Victims* on the Palestinian tragedy are both polemical but a bit of a relief after the knotty arguments in *Orientalism*.

Noam Chomsky (1983) *The Fateful Triangle — The United States, Israel and Palestinians* London: Pluto
It's biased, it's weird, it's intellectually stimulating. Don't take this one into Israel.

COOKERY

Arto der Haroutunian (1982) *Middle Eastern Cookery* London: Pan

If you are into your cooking and want to do a bit of pre-trip reading, this is very highly recommended. As well as recipes, it contains all sorts of snippets of history, proverbs and anecdotes. Also, the recipes actually turn out to be edible which is more than can be said for a lot of Middle Eastern cookbooks.

EARLY TRAVELLERS

In many ways all the books here are obsolete, but in terms of getting a feel for the region these are very often the best books for a seriously interested traveller. It helps to see where people came from, not just a snapshot of today.

E.W. Lane (1944) *Modern Egyptians* London: J.M. Dent

This one is a sort of perma classic. It also includes the quickest way of picking up dozy/dreamy student girls short of carrying a pack of tarot cards (p. 267 in the Everyman edition). It contains a quite enormous amount of ephemeral information about Egypt in the early nineteenth century, far more than is necessary surely.

Sir Richard Burton (1986) *Personal Narrative of a Pilgrimage to Al Madinah and Meccah* London: 2 vols, Darf

This is probably the best one of Burton's to start with – it is one of his least obviously insane ones. Burton is a love him or hate him author. I rate him pretty good, others hate his bombastic discursive style.

Charles Doughty (1979) *Travels in Arabia Deserta* New York: 2
   vols, Dover
The book for serious readers. Nothing is like *Arabia Deserta.* The
prose style takes some getting used to, but if you want an in-depth
appreciation of Arab life at the turn of the century, this cannot
be bettered. Penguin published a much shortened version, but it
lacks the grandeur of the full text. More portable though. This
is unfortunately out of print.

Charles Kinglake (1982) *Eothen* London: Century
This has never been out of print, and quite right too. Very funny
indeed, a cynical tour of the Middle East complete with ironic
musings on whether it would be fun to have a servant killed and
bizarre encounters in the Sinai desert. A laugh out loud in public
number, even now.

FICTION

Arabian Nights (1982) London: Century, or Oxford: OUP
An excellent compilation of traditional Arab tales; because it
has been so often bowdlerised, there is a residual impression that
this is a children's book. Rubbish! Get an unexpurgated copy and
lech along with Scheherazade. Can't beat it – booze, babes, dirty
tricks and dirty jokes.

James Morier (1989) *The Adventures of Hajji Baba of Ispahan* 2
   vols, revised edition, Thornhill: Tynron Press
Tremendous book. One of the funniest written on the Middle
East. Hajji Baba is the most unpleasing hero: venal, boastful,
lecherous and conceited, but his adventures are just splendid.
Not to be missed.

TWENTIETH-CENTURY FICTION

There is so much of this that any recommendations are entirely personal. I like ones that touch on the melancholy of life, but can see that many readers might prefer less gloomy holiday reading.

Emile Habiby (1985) *The Adventures of Saeed the Ill Fated Pessoptimist* London: Zed Books

Waguib Ghali (1987) *Beer in the Snooker Club* London: Serpent's Tail

Naguib Mahfouz (1983) *Miramar* London: Doubleday
   Ghali gives a more metropolitan view of Cairo than Mahfouz and is highly recommended. Mahfouz is one of these novelists who is more often bought than read, which is a pity.

Paul Bowles (1990) *The Sheltering Sky* London: Paladin Grafton

Mohammed Mrabet (1986) *Love with a Few Hairs* trans. P. Bowles London: Arena

M'Hashish (1988) trans. P. Bowles London: Peter Owen

The Sheltering Sky is a deeply oppressive book that should be required north African reading. Even odder and more difficult to get hold of are the tales of Mohammed Mrabet, taped and translated by Bowles. Weird ones.

GUIDE BOOKS

The most commonly used travellers' guides are the Rough Guides and the Lonely Planet series. Fodor and Berlitz guides tend to be more geared to relatively well-off travellers, though worth picking up if you see them second-hand. Insight Guides are good for pictures — this makes them very popular with the locals of the country you are visiting and to that extent they are certainly worth considering. Rough Guides are, let's face it, worthy. They have one other major drawback and that is an odd one. They are all written to a consistent length so the one on Tunisia is about the same length as the one on Egypt, which is plainly ridiculous. There is a certain encyclopaedic earnestness about the Rough Guides that can make them a tiresome read. The one on Morocco is particularly lifeless.

Lonely Planet guides are sharply written and one or two laughs can be had. They don't get too dewy-eyed or romanticise disgusting customs in the way Rough Guides do. In purely practical terms they are relatively robustly bound and are less likely to come apart than a Rough Guide, which tends to fall to bits after about a month of travelling, less if you throw them against too many walls in irritation.

Best are

Tom Brosnahan (1994) *Middle East* Lonely Planet
Damien Simonis (1993) *Jordan and Syria* Lonely Planet

Another point to notice is that Arabs read these books too, particularly Arab crooks/businessmen, so recommended restaurants and hotels tend to become magnets for local rip-off artists.

MAPS

Those produced locally tend to exaggerate the importance of places, the facilities available and the state of the roads. This can be important if you are travelling to out-of-the-way places. If somewhere on a map is marked as having a petrol station, there is no guarantee that this will in fact turn out to exist when you get there. Town maps produced in the Middle East are simply fanciful and are no use whatsoever for navigation; the worst are produced in Yemen and are worth seeking out for their blatant incomprehensibility.

One of the best general maps to consider taking is the Hallwag *Turkey Near East* at 1:2500000. This covers a quite typical long trip in the Middle East that is from Turkey round through Jordan and/or Israel and into Egypt, all on one fairly hardwearing sheet. This does make a difference, as taking three or four maps of different scales gets a bit confusing.

ANTI-BIBLIOGRAPHY

There are a great number of books written on the Middle East and, as many of them seem to be exceedingly expensive, choosing what to spend your hard-earned pennies on is difficult enough. If you lay out money on a book that turns out to be unreadable, you may quite properly feel resentful. There are certain types of title to be wary of:

'And' Titles

These tend to link two unrelated words in an attempt to grab the attention. Titles like *The Arabs: Sensuality and Responsibility*, or *Visions and Eras: The Middle East Today, Tomorrow and Last Thursday* are giveaways that you could be laying out money on something which may be a speculative yawn.

':' Titles

Examples like *Arab Women: Behind the Harem Doors*, *Arab Minorities: Under The Thumb*, *The Arabs: Under the Sideboard*.

Anything that has a colon followed by a preposition of place is a risky buy.

'Inside' Titles

Inside the Arab Mind, etc., etc. These titles suggest you are going to get the low-down on the subject – you much more often just get the low-down on the author.

If you are choosing a travel book, words in the title which should put that book fairly far down the queue are: 'Among' or 'Journey' (*especially* journey to the heart of anywhere/thing). 'Up' and 'through' are less dangerous warning signals but, if coupled with an obviously silly definition, should be regarded with suspicion. Thus hypothetically the simple *Travel through Oman* is less likely to be hysterically awful than *Journey through the Land of the Fire Goat*.

'With' titles

Some of these should have health warnings. Obviously insane ones are easy enough to avoid; you'd need to be pretty daft to lay out twenty quid on *From Tel Aviv to Cairo with my Ukulele*. But anyone who defines where they are going by what they take with them is, to be charitable, starting off with the wrong idea.

MAGAZINES

Well I take great pleasure in recommending a completely unfashionable read. *The National Geographic* has two advantages. Firstly it is available in every library this side of a mobile van and secondly it is illegal for charity shops not to stock them. As they are indexed along the spines and never cost much more than twenty pence it is worth running through even a large pile of these to see if where you are thinking of going gets a mention. The pictures are always excellent, sometimes the prose too. Travel bores always criticise them for being over-optimistic, but why not start off with an optimistic attitude? It's the only way to travel.

 Started in 1992 by Kevin Williamson, with help from established young authors Duncan McLean and Gordon Legge, Rebel Inc. magazine set out with the intention of promoting and publishing what was seen then as a new wave of young urban Scottish writers who were kicking back against the literary mainstream.

The Rebel Inc book imprint intends to develop the magazine ethos through publishing accessible as well as challenging texts aimed at extending the domain of counter-culture literature.

The first four titles point towards the future direction of Rebel Inc

Children of Albion Rovers
Irvine Welsh, Alan Warner, Gordon Legge,
James Meek, Laura J. Hird, Paul Reekie
A collection of novellas from six of the best young writers to emerge from Scotland in the 90s - £8.99

Hunger
Knut Hamsun
A new translation by Sverre Lyngstad
with an introduction by Duncan Mclean
Classic first novel by the Nobel prize-winning Norwegian - £6.99

Young Adam
Alexander Trocchi
Introduced by John Pringle
Seminal first work from the Scottish Beat writer - £6.99

Drugs and the Party Line
Kevin Williamson
Introduction by Irvine Welsh
A polemic on the politics of recreational drug use - £4.99

The above are available from all good book shops
or can be ordered directly from:

Canongate Books, 14 High St, Edinburgh EH1 1TE
Tel 0131 557 5111 Fax 0131 557 5211
email canongate@post.almac.co.uk

All forms of payment are accepted and p&p is free to any address in the U.K. Please specify if you want to join the Rebel Inc. mailing list.

DRUGS AND THE PARTY LINE

KEVIN WILLIAMSON
WITH AN INTRODUCTION BY IRVINE WELSH

The use of recreational drugs has become the subject of an unprecedented national debate. Unfortunately the outbreak of media hysteria following the death of Leah Betts and others has provoked leading politicians into declaring a war on drugs.

Illegal drugs have been described as the new "enemy within" and drug-users equated with "a medieval plague". Any semblance of rational debate has been buried beneath the hysteria. The first casualty of any war is truth and for the war against drugs this has been no different.

Drugs and the Party Line aims to cut through the hysteria, hype and myths surrounding the use of recreational drugs in an accessible and informed way. Sticking to the facts, *Drugs and the Party Line* asks the questions that the politicians should really be addressing.

Unlike most books on the subject of drugs, *Drugs and the Party Line* not only answers these questions but puts forward a full political manifesto for changing existing drug laws based on progressive drug-specific policies of harm reduction, decriminalisation of drug-users, plus controlled availability for some drugs.